Elizabeth Bedell Benjamin

Brightside

Elizabeth Bedell Benjamin

Brightside

ISBN/EAN: 9783337155063

Printed in Europe, USA, Canada, Australia, Japan

Cover: Foto ©Thomas Meinert / pixelio.de

More available books at **www.hansebooks.com**

BRIGHTSIDE.

BY

E. BEDELL BENJAMIN,

AUTHOR OF "ELEVEN MONTHS IN HOREB," AND "THE CHURCH IN
THE WILDERNESS."

NEW YORK:

ROBERT CARTER AND BROTHERS,

530 BROADWAY.

1873.

ST. JOHNLAND STEREOTYPE FOUNDRY,
SUFFOLK COUNTY, N. Y.

Brightside:

A little story of happy days,

for

Addie, Fannie, Lulu,

BERTIE, ELLIE

and

Daisy and Aline,

from

COUSIN LILLY.

CONTENTS.

BRIGHTSIDE.

I.

About Happy Christmas.

TWO little white beds, in a large and bright nursery, contained, on Christmas morning, the little boy and girl of whose nice times I intend to tell you.

One little brown head popped up from the pillow, just as dawn was turning from gray to very pale yellow, and keeping a pair of bright eyes very straight in their direction towards the other bed, their owner exclaimed, "Mary, Mary, wake up, it's Happy Christmas, and I know the stockings are full, but I haven't looked."

"Oh, so they are! Happy Christmas, Harry.

Bring yours right over here," exclaimed the little sister whom Henry had wakened ; " I've got mine down."

One jump and two twinkles of two white feet, brought Henry and his stocking to Mary's bed, and in a few minutes their contents were examined. Balls, books, and all sorts of little things that could be thought of by loving parents, were found in them. " Isn't it splendid ?" exclaimed Henry, " and more to come besides ; I do love Christmas !"

These were happy children, they always saw the bright side of everything, and they talked merrily of their new playthings, and of the pleasant day which they felt sure they would have, for my story is about little children who were very seldom naughty or sick, and who were glad and happy about everything. If the sun shone they liked that, if the birds sang and the trees made little happy noises with their leaves, they liked that, and if the clouds covered the sun, and the rain came down, they said " it was just the day to

stay at home and do up odds and ends."
These "odds and ends" consisted in mending
playthings, arranging papa's newspapers and
books, upsetting mamma's work-basket and
putting it in order again, "cleaning house" in
the dolls' house, playing tenpins in the attic,
making gingerbread in the nursery, and, if it
was not vacation, saying lessons to mamma.

But I must not leave them any longer sitting
on the bed, for Christmas was always a
very busy day. They had begun to try a hymn,
which was to be sung at mamma's door, when
the nurse came in. I wish you could have
seen that nurse! She was as black as coffee
burnt a great deal too much, she had very
shiny black eyes in the whitest whites of
eyes you ever saw, she had an uncommonly
nice nose and mouth, and very white teeth.
Then, she wore a red and yellow turban, very
clean and very bright, it looked like a flower
bed, and nodded about, when she talked, in the
happiest way. Her head and turban had a
very large body to hold them, but what with

the clean calico dress of a dozen colors, and
the white apron, it was a pleasant picture to
look upon, and one that every one liked, from
the little children on the bed, to the little
lame girl at the mill.

"Happy 'Krismas, chil'n. Blessed good
times dis day when de hebbenly Master came
to brighten up dis world."

"Happy Christmas, Minny; what did you
get in your stocking? hurry and tell us, because we've got to go and sing."

"Blessins on you, dear chil'n, you can't
wake de Missis yet, and you must be dressed
'fore you go, so I'll tell you what I had. Dere
was a box full of scissors, and a box of pins,
'cause you must allers gib pins after you gib
scissors. Dem was from de Missis, den I had
vayrus tings from the suvvant girls, and a
new silk turban from Minny's dear little boy."

"Oh," said Henry, "wasn't it bright? just
as bright as—as a rainbow."

"Yes," said Minny, "bright as any rainbow
down on dis land, de hebbenly rainbows is

kinder clearer color" (for Minny was careful how she compared earthly things with heavenly), "and you is a dear good boy to think of Minny. Den I had a nice new Bible, wid de beautifullest picture of de angels singing to de shepherds dat glory song."

"I gave you that," exclaimed Mary. "I'm so glad you liked that picture."

"Tank you for gibing it to me, dear. I tink it de most glorysome picture in de world. De blessed angels comin down in de dark still night, and singing to de shepherds dat glory song!" And then Minny could restrain her feelings no longer, but burst out in a glory song of her own, the children joining with her striving to follow her heart of praise as she sang :

> Glory be to God on high,
> Glory on dis morning.
> Hebbenly angels coming nigh,
> Glory on dis morning.
> Singing, "Peace, good-will to men,"
> Glory on dis morning.
> Happy times on earth be den,
> Glory *ebery* morning.

One long look she gave towards the sun rising in a mass of golden clouds. It seemed to her a glimpse of heavenly light. Then remembering the duties of the day, she exclaimed : "Now chil'n, let us pray to de good Lord, and den we'll be ready for 'Krismas day."

They kneeled down as they did each day, one on each side of her. Mary prayed her little prayer first, then Henry prayed his, after which Minny said, "Hear dem, good Lord," and then the three prayed "Our Father," all speaking together, and ending with "All this we ask for Jesus' sake. Amen."

This was Minny's little service. I may not tell you about it every day, but it was always attended to the first thing in the morning. The Bible verses which the children learned were said to their mother. After their prayers, Henry went to a little room next to the nursery, where he dressed, while Minny helped Mary. On this morning, Mary was dressed in a very clear bright blue merino, made high in the neck, her dress was short and she had white stockings and black gaiter boots, and these, by Henry's especial wish, had blue buttons, for he was always much interested in what Mary wore. Henry had dark blue pantaloons and a blue cloth sacque with bright buttons and a leather belt. A white collar turned down, and white cuffs turned up. They both had dark, curling hair, cut short, brown eyes and very red cheeks. Somehow everything in this house was bright, everybody's eyes shone, and there were more rosy cheeks than I have ever seen in any other family. I never heard any reason for it, but always supposed it was because every one was happy.

After they were dressed, they went on tiptoe and hand in hand. to the door of the room on the other side of the hall, and there began their Christmas hymn. They had clear voices and sang, as well as little children could sing, the beautiful old hymn :

"While shepherds watched their flocks by night,
All seated on the ground,

The Angel of the Lord came down,
    And glory shone around."

Every verse was sung. Papa and mamma
listened, with hearts full of praise, to the dear
voices of their precious children. Minny
listened too, pausing in her work and praying
in her loving heart, " Good Lord, bless dem
chil'n." The servants heard in the kitchen
too, and happy Christmas thoughts brightened
their day's work.

When the hymn was over, the door opened,
Christmas greetings were given, and " dear
mamma and papa" kissed and thanked their
little singing birds, as they called them.

" Oh, mamma, we had such lovely presents ;
we thank you and papa ever so much, and do
you think grandma will come, and will we
have our basket too, and— ?"

" Stop my boy," exclaimed his father ; " I do
think grandma will come, and you shall have
your basket too, only let us have breakfast,
and make our plans afterwards. Come in till
mamma is ready."

Mamma was soon ready, and having heard Henry and Mary repeat the verses they had learned for the morning, they all went down to the breakfast room, talking and laughing, in their usual happy way. This room was small and sunshiny, with a bright crackling wood fire, making everything cheerful ; a nice breakfast, and what the children thought better than all, the whole room was gay with evergreens and red berries.

"Oh," said Mary, " it's just like the woods ; don't you think it is a picnic, Henry?"

" I think it is nicer than the nicest picnic in the world," said Henry ; "it's mamma and papa, and Christmas, and home, and grandma coming, and I'm so hungry, I can't wait another minute."

" That is extremely like a picnic," said his father ; "every one is hungry in the woods."

"Yes," said Henry, "that's the fun of it ; that dinner on the ground and everybody all in a heap, but I like winter best, it's so nice and cold, and it's such fun to slide and skate."

"Oh, Henry," replied Mary, "I 'member you said exactly that last summer. I don't mean about the skating, but that you liked summer the best because it was so nice and warm."

"Did I?" Well, you must not keep remembering things; I believe I did like the summer, but I had not had this winter then."

To Henry's surprise, his mother quietly left the head of the table, and going to him, kissed his broad fair brow, and without saying anything returned to her seat.

"Why, mamma, thank you dear; but what made you do that?"

His father laughed at his surprise, and said, "Mamma is glad that you are happy, my boy. Now listen to me a few minutes. As soon as we have finished breakfast, we will go to the chapel where the Sunday-school children are to sing the Christmas anthem, and to have a short service. The church will be closed on account of Mr. Clark, our clergyman, having been summoned to see his father, who is ill. After that we will return home and prepare our own gifts which have not already been sent.   Then grandma will come, and we will have our own 'basket,' and our quiet evening afterwards.   Do you like this plan ?"

"Oh yes, papa, it's a lovely little pro ham," said Mary.

" A lovely what ?" asked Henry.

" A pro ham.   I mean that thing that tells what is coming," explained Mary, looking a little confused.   She was very fond of using new or hard words, and had already had some experience in making mistakes.

"A programme, dear," said mamma.   "The word is quite right, only you did not pronounce it correctly."   The loving look that her mother gave, helped Mary to bear Henry's merry laugh, when he said :

" You're such a jolly little sister !"

"Now go to Minny," said mamma, "and tell her to put on your high boots, for the snow is quite deep.   Run—ten minutes for preparations, such talkers as you both are ! You leave very little time for dressing."

Ten minutes for boots and wraps, a merry plunge into the snow, exclamations of delight at the dark evergreens hanging full of snow balls, and at the frosted silver effect of the sunlight on the surface of the snow, a run down to the gate of the park, a few moments waiting for papa and mamma, then a more sober walk, and the little chapel was reached.

II.

About Christmas at the Sunday-school.

THE scholars were in their places and looked very bright and happy. Mr. Watkins, the superintendent of the school, explained the absence of their beloved pastor, and spoke of his regret at not being able to be with his people on this joyful day. He then read a portion of the service, after which one of the Christmas hymns was sung, and then he told the children that he had selected some of the questions from their lessons of the previous year, which were on the subject of the Saviour's birth, and that he wished them to reply all together.

The questions and answers were as follows, the children standing during the recitation :

" Who appeared to the shepherds on the night when our Saviour was born ?"

" And, lo, the angel of the Lord came upon them."

" What did the angel say to the shepherds ?"

" Fear not : for, behold, I bring you good tidings of great joy, which shall be to all people."

" What were the good tidings which the angel brought ?"

" Unto you is born this day a Saviour, which is Christ the Lord."

" What chorus of great joy was sung by the hosts of heaven as the good tidings were told ?"

" And suddenly there was with the angel a multitude of the heavenly host praising God, and saying :

" Glory to God in the highest, and on earth peace, good-will towards men."

" Did the shepherds go to seek the Saviour ?"

" And it came to pass, as the angels were gone away from them into heaven, the shep-

herds said one to another, Let us now go
even unto Bethlehem, and see this thing
which is come to pass, which the Lord hath
made known unto us. And they came with
haste, and found Mary and Joseph, and the
babe lying in a manger."

"In what words had the birth of Christ in
Bethlehem been foretold by the prophet
Micah ?"

"But thou Bethlehem Ephratah, though
thou be little among the thousands of Judah,
yet out of thee shall He come forth that
is to be Ruler in Israel."

"Where was the town of Bethlehem ?"

One little boy answered : "Six miles south
of Jerusalem ; it was built on a hill."

"What is the meaning of the word Bethlehem ?"

All the children knew this, and answered,
"House of Bread."

"What made this a very appropriate name
for the birthplace of the Saviour ?"

"Jesus said unto them, I am the bread of life."

" How was Jesus the bread of life ?"

" The bread of God is He which cometh down from heaven and giveth life unto the world."

" How did Jesus give life to the world ?"

" He that believeth on me hath everlasting life.   I am that bread of life."

" Why was Bethlehem called little among the thousands of Judah ?"

" It was a small town, compared with some of the large cities of Judah."

" What had the prophet Micah said that Jesus would be ?"

" A Ruler in Israel."

" What had the angel said He would be ?"

" A Saviour, which is Christ the Lord."

" Why was Jesus called a Saviour ?"

" Because He came to save His people from their sins."

" Did He save them from anything besides the punishment of their sins ?"

" From the power of sin," said one voice.

" From being sinners," said another.

" From wanting to sin," said another.

" Yes, dear children," said Mr. Watkins ; " you are all right, the love of the Saviour, and the love of sin, cannot be in the same heart. He came to save you from *sin.* Sin in itself, and sin in its consequences."

" What is the meaning of Christ, and why is this also a name of the Saviour ?"

" Christ means, Anointed, and Jesus was anointed to be a Prince and a Saviour."

" Why was He called the Lord ?"

" Because He was the Lord of heaven and earth," said several voices.

One little girl said, " Because He *is* the Lord of heaven and earth."

" Right," said Mr. Watkins ; " both are right, ' was ' and ' is.' Now give me a text for both words."

" Who was, and is, and is to come," said the little girl who had spoken last.

" Now, children, who can repeat what the prophet Isaiah said would be some of the names of our Saviour ?"

"His name shall be called Wonderful, Counsellor, The Mighty God, The Everlasting Father, The Prince of Peace."

"Did this mean that Jesus Christ would be called by all these names, or that they described His character or His official work?"

"I think the names told what He was and what He did," said several voices.

"Who went to see Jesus besides the shepherds?"

"Behold there came wise men from the East to Jerusalem, saying, where is He that is born King of the Jews?"

"Why did they inquire at Jerusalem?"

"They thought the King would be born in the capital city."

"Did Herod the king know how to answer them?"

"No; for when he had gathered the chief priests and scribes of the people together, he demanded of them where Christ should be born."

"Who were the chief priests and scribes?"

The children hesitated, as this was one of the questions they had not learned, therefore, Mr. Watkins asked :

" To what nation did they belong ?"

" The Jewish nation," was readily answered.

" What were the duties of the priests ?"

" To offer gifts and sacrifices and to attend to the services in the Temple."

" What were the duties of the scribes ?"

" To teach the people, and to copy the holy books."

" How could the chief priests and scribes know about this expected King ?"

" The priests read the Scriptures which told of Him, and the scribes copied them so often that they knew how many letters each book contained, so that they at once answered in the words of the Prophet Micah, that their Ruler was to be born in Bethlehem of Judah." This answer was given by one of the larger boys.

" Now, children," said Mr. Watkins, " you have answered correctly, and in a manner

that proves you have understood the teach-
ings in regard to our Saviour. I would like
to hear more on the subject, for it comes to
us each year with new interest, but there are
other enjoyments of the day, from which I will
not detain you. I have but one word to leave
with you. Each one of you is a part of the
world which Christ Jesus came to save. Do
not fail to seek His love, to place yourselves
in His fold. Let the Saviour, heralded by
angels, born in Bethlehem, worshipped by
wise men, be *your* Saviour, *your* King, *your*
Prince, *your* Lord, and *your* God."

"We will now sing the Christmas anthem,
and after it you will receive your gifts."

The words that were sung were those of
the angels :

" Glory be to God in the highest,
And on earth
Peace, good-will to men."

The music of the Sunday-school was generally sung in four parts, the voices being
divided in this way, each part having a leader,

but on this occasion they all sang the same part, the music being written in unison, and sung in a subdued, solemn tone. The effect was very impressive, and seemed as if heard from a distance. Music was carefully cultivated in the school, and the singing was always so good, that many of the congregation came on Sundays to hear the closing hymn.

Henry and Mary were not members of the Sunday-school. As Mr. Montgomerie had time to instruct them, he preferred to teach them at home, but they enjoyed singing with the school, and on this occasion united with great interest.

Before the distribution of the gifts, Mr. Watkins said : " My dear children, the books which are given to you to-day are all alike. They are not prizes. Those who have been inattentive will receive the same as those who have been punctual to every duty for the year. At other seasons you have prizes, this day you have free gifts from your teachers, *because we love you.*   Now come for them in the order in which you are seated."

The scholars went quietly to the table, and while they were receiving their gifts, Mr. and Mrs. Montgomerie and their children returned home.

III.

About the Gifts Given.

THE next thing on the "pro ham," as Mary called it, was to send the Christmas gifts to the village, and to the many poor families in the neighborhood.

On returning from the chapel, they found everything that was needed for putting them up, placed by the careful Minny on the dining-room table.

There were baskets, rolls of paper, balls of twine, cards to write names on, and pens and ink to write with ; then there were turkeys, — and apple-sauce, and other nice things for dinners, some baskets of flowers, and some of grapes, all to be arranged under the direction of Mrs. Montgomerie. Most of the parcels had been put up before, but as Mary wisely remarked, the "eating things *must* be 'tended to on Christmas day."

The dinner baskets were soon arranged, and for each family some especial remembrance.

" Mary dear," said mamma, " what have you for Nora, the little lame girl? I do not see your parcel."

" Here mamma, a doll and my picture of the two children with evergreens from the wood."

" Put it in this corner of the basket," said mamma, " and the blue flannel sacque for her, in this white paper—there, that will do nicely. Now Henry, tie this card on the handle, ' Nora Herndon. Happy Christmas for a patient little girl.'"

" Now, mamma, please give me the cards for the other baskets. Here is one for Madame Louville, who is she?" asked Henry.

" The French lady, dear. I have her basket all ready. It contains something more delicate than a turkey, and some flowers, which she will like, even if she cannot see them. Keep this cotton over them, for they have just been brought from the green-house."

"She is the blind lady who is to teach us French, don't you 'member, Henry?" said Mary, as she ran to the hall with her little arms full of parcels.

"Now, mamma, I have them all," said Henry, putting on his fur collar and warm gloves. Tom is here, and I will go at once. Is there anything for the poor-house people?"

"No, dear, grandma has taken care of the dinner for them. You are only to leave these flowers for that old organ-grinder; perhaps they may bring him a memory of his old home."

Frolic, Henry's pony, was shaking his bells at the door, while Minny and Tom were packing the baskets and parcels in the box-sleigh, a freight of blessings for the poor and the sick. All of which Henry and Tom, the coachman, promised to deliver carefully.

"Be sure to be at home by two o'clock,

Henry," cried Mary, " for grandma is coming then."

" Yes, dear, good-bye," and Henry and Tom, and Frolic, and the presents, went off in a jubilee of sleigh-bells.

As Mary closed the door, she said very gravely, " Mamma, I'm very glad we are a 'nevolent family."

" Yes, dear," said her mother, trying not to laugh ; " it is a great happiness to be able to give comfort to those who need it. We need not talk of what we do ; but while Minny puts up the papers and strings, you and I will see if everything is in order."

As Minny passed, she said, in a low voice : " More blessed to gib dan to receive, missis you know."

" Yes, Minny," replied Mrs. Montgomerie ; " but we only give of our abundance."

" I tink missis, de same heart would make you gib, if you was eber so poor," replied Minny, who well knew how much time and strength Mrs. Montgomerie spent in finding

out those who really needed help, and in trying to help them in the best way.

" Here, mamma," said Mary, pulling after
her a long wreath; " where is this to go ?
I can help you, mamma. I don't know where
papa is."

" He has gone off mysteriously about some
Christmas work, I suppose," replied her
mother, as she fastened the wreath.

" Mamma, may I have these red berries,
and may I do just what I like with them ?"
presently asked Mary, who had found a stray
bunch of them.

" You may, my little girl, and when you
have finished, come up into my room. I am
going to dress for dinner."

" Minny," said Mary, " give me a needle
and thread, please. I am going to string
them for mamma's head-dress."

This was soon done, and mamma was persuaded to consent to Mary's addition to her
toilet. Mary, arranging them with coral pins,
and other devices of her own, pronounced her

mother " too lovely for anything. Just like a
beautiful Mrs. Santaclaus," and ran to find
papa, to ask his opinion, but she failed to do
so, and told her mother, " papa has gone off
seriously about something."

" What do you mean, dear?" asked her
mother. " Do you mean gravely?"

" Oh, no, mamma, I mean the way we all
do at Christmas. Seriously, no, I mean 'steri-
ously, the word you said," explained Mary.

Mamma explained " mysteriously " to her,
which was the word she tried to say, and Mary
learned to pronounce it. By that time papa
had returned, and he and Mary had a fine game
of ball before Henry came home. The large
hall on the second floor was a fine place for
a game, and the new balls seemed very glad
to have an opportunity to jump and leap about.
I think Mrs. Montgomerie was a little glad
when the noisy game was over, which was as
soon as Frolic's sleigh bells were heard at
the door.

Henry had performed his part of the day's

work like a man. In some places, he had
held the little gay pony, while Tom delivered
the parcels, in others, where there was a message, Tom had taken care of Frolic, while
Henry delivered the parcel. He reached
Brightside (which I had forgotten to tell you,
was the name of Mr. Montgomerie's place)
sometime before grandma arrived, and had a
great deal to tell Mary about his excursion.

While they were talking, Minny reminded
them that it was time to dress for dinner ;
but Henry told Mary about Nora, and her
delight with the doll and picture, and about
Sorella, the organ-grinder's little girl, and
Jocko, her monkey. Mary had sent Sorella a
blue ribbon, with a little bell, to tie around
Jocko's neck, and Henry tried to describe the
comical faces that Jocko made, and how he
listened to the bell, and his delight, when he
found that striking it with his paw made it
ring.

After they were dressed, and had looked at
all the wreaths and berries, excepting those

in the closed parlor, and had admired mamma's head-dress, they went to the hall window to look for grandma. I must begin another chapter, to tell you about her.

IV.

About the Gifts Received.

THE favorite playmate of Henry and Mary
was grandmamma. She played house,
better than any one else, she was wonderful
at tenpins and ball, she understood the mys-
teries of Henry's railroad trains and his time-
tables as well as of Mary's dolls and their
extensive toilets, she could tell stories on
every known subject, and invent them on the
unknown. She loved dogs and birds, horses,
cows, chickens, ducks and turkeys, and they
all loved her. She had new plans for amusements when the old ones failed, and always
seemed to be inventing them for herself, and
to be persuading the others to try them. In
short, she was the "dearest, best grandmamma

in the world," as Mary told her whenever she saw her.

This dear grandmamma was Mr. Montgomerie's mother. She was not tall, not nearly as tall as her son, she had the same kind of brown hair, and eyes, and bright face as the members of the family at Brightside, and the same happy nature. Grandmamma lived five miles the other side of the village, about nine miles from Brightside, and her home was named Burnside. It was a large farm, with all the delightful things that farms always have, such as a dairy, with bright pans of milk and cream, a poultry yard, with little yellow chickens, and little brown ducks, an old apple orchard with odd crooked trees, so nice and easy to climb, fields of wheat and corn, which were plowed with shiny oxen with long horns, and a garden in which grew all sorts of vegetables for well people to eat, and herbs to make tea for sick people to drink. There was a wagon house, where it was delightful to play stage coach, and a tool house, where was the best place in the world to play store. Then, directly through the dear old apple orchard, there ran a stream of water, very wide and noisy after a rain, and in the spring, and very gentle and peaceable in the warm summer months. This stream had several small waterfalls, and three dear little islands, on one of them was a tree under which Henry intended sometime to build a cottage.

In the winter, there was one part of the stream which froze over very smoothly, so that the children could skate, and there was no fear of breaking through and drowning, because the water was too shallow for that dreadful thing to happen. I have not told you all about this farm, but quite enough to prove to you that no other place, except their own home, could have more attractions for the children. Grandmamma lived there alone, entertaining a great deal of company, and occupying many hours each day with the poor and sick people who needed care. Henry and

Mary were always welcome, although she could not always play with them. They knew exactly what to do when she was occupied, understanding each other perfectly. They did not tease her, but when she was ready to play with them their happy voices seemed happier than before, and their bright eyes danced more merrily.

Of course, Christmas day would not have been complete if grandmamma had not come to dine at Brightside. She could not come until nearly three o'clock, because she always made a Christmas festival for the poor-house people, superintending their dinner and making them happy in various ways. Among them was the old organ-grinder with his grand-child, and his monkey. The old man, when playing on his organ, in the streets of the village, had fallen down with a stroke of paralysis. They were taken to the poor-house, because no one knew what else to do with them.

Mrs. Montgomerie heard of it, and induced

the managers to permit them all to remain. The little girl and the monkey were great favorites, and amused the sick people so much, that the doctor said he thought such entertainments ought to be introduced into every hospital. They were often sent for to the village, to amuse those who were confined to their rooms. Many a little child, with a face thin and sharpened by suffering, was cheered and helped to get well, by a visit from the organ grinder's Bambino and monkey. The doctor called Sorella, the grand-child, "his assistant." The old man was well taken care of, and, in his broken English, tried to express his gratitude, but it was hard to understand him, and as he slept most of the time, very little could be done for him.

Mrs. Montgomerie returned home after the poor-house dinner, so that it was nearly an hour after Henry reached Brightside, before the distant ring of her sleigh bells was heard.

"There she comes," exclaimed Mary. "I know the jingle lingle dingle."

"Yes," replied Henry. "She is by the brook, now over the bridge—now past the chapel—now to the gate—I left it open for her—here she comes! jingle ingle ingle— whoa, old Major and Minor."

They threw open the door, and " Ah, you dear dear grandma," and " How are my darling children?" and " James, take that basket in carefully," and " Grandma, let me take your muff and cape—or will you go up-stairs? Here are papa and mamma!"

"Happy Christmas! dear mother. I was afraid we should have to go to the poor-house for you."

" No, indeed, my children, my heart came here and I came with it. What a magnificent drive I had! how beautiful the house looks, and—why! my dear daughter, you are dressed in Christmas berries, too. How becoming they are!"

Mary whispered to Henry, " I knew it. I'm so glad, and Henry, did you see that basket?"

" Yes, I saw, don't say anything. I think

James tried to get it in secretly; oh, isn't Christmas fun? It's such a jumble."

The jumble cleared up a little, and they were soon comfortably partaking of such a Christmas dinner as the Brightside cook prided herself upon. There was a good deal of merry talk, and many interesting incidents from the dinner which grandma had given her pensioners. Mamma asked how grandma's old cook, Lucy, who had lived with her for thirty years, could accomplish so much?

"Why," said grandma, laughing, "it was not really more than preparing for a dinner party, and Lucy would feel greatly offended if I thought she were too old for that. I asked her if she could do this for me, and she said: 'Certain, Missis, if you'll give me an extra, for I never was teached to be druv,' so I gave her an 'extra,' and the dinner was a great success."

"She is an odd old creature," said Mr. Montgomerie. "Do you remember, mother, when I gave her an umbrella for a Christmas present, how she insisted upon carrying her old one, saying,'You don't spec me to carry my new umbrella when it rains.'"

There were many other reminiscences of Mr. Montgomerie's early days, during which Lucy had been rather tyrannical, but when at last he was married, she had pronounced him "the most ladylike gemman she ever seed," and now prided herself on having been the chief cause of his success in life.

The children were much amused with all this, and Mary had some trouble to keep even moderately quiet. Once she replied to a little reminding look from her mother, "Yes, dear mamma, I *am* trying to be very still." Henry laughed at her failure, and it reminded grand-mamma to tell them about the old lady who took her cat to church, with a pitcher of milk to keep her quiet ; at last the pussy got her head fastened in the pitcher, and ran breaking and crashing it down the aisle, the old lady exclaiming, "Oh, pussy, be quiet! oh, I spoke in church. Oh, I spoke again, dear, dear ! I keep speaking all the time." They laughed at this, and I am afraid Mary would have had to talk about it, but the blazing plum pudding was placed on the table, and she was too much afraid of it to think of anything else. She whispered to Henry, "*Must* we swallow the blaze?" This was too much for Henry, and his merry shout of laughter made his papa ask him if he too were trying to be quiet?

"Oh, papa, please excuse me," he said, "but Mary is so very funny."

"I did not mean to be," said Mary, "but I don't like that fiery mountain, and I don't want to eat it." By this time the "fiery mountain" was blown out, Mary was reconciled to the pudding, and the remainder of the dessert was peacefully eaten.

Then the brown eyes began to turn towards the parlor, and papa proposed they should go at once to their own Christmas basket.

"You see, grandma," said Mary, "we are very 'nevolent, and it puts our presents off till nearly dark time."

"That is inconvenient," replied grardma; "but there is so much to do on Christmas day. I do not see how it can be helped."

The parlor doors were thrown open, and screams of delight proved that mamma's preparations were a success. The brightest of wreaths of berries and evergreens ornamented every part of the room. Flowers were in every vase, and under the chandelier, which was festooned with greens and bright with lights, stood the figure of a very old woman. Mamma introduced her as Dame Santaclaus. She held an umbrella over her head, another was her walking-stick, on her back was one basket, on her arm was another; she drew after her by ropes around her waist, a velocipede, a wheelbarrow and doll's bedstead; skates and and a large stereoscope were hanging from her neck. The old lady was much bent over with her burdens, but her face beamed with just such smiles as those with which her old husband illumined the Christmas nights.

Henry and Mary danced around her in

delight ; they could make as much noise as they pleased now. Mamma said first one and then the other could take off her load, and she would read the addresses for them. Mary began with the umbrella that was in the hand of the old dame. It was of dark green silk, with an ivory handle carved in a dog's head, and Henry's name upon the dog's collar. Papa gave it to him, to carry when it rained, not to leave it at home as Lucy did. The other one was dark blue—with a bird's head for a handle and Mary's name upon it. The skates were next taken down, a new pair for each from grandma. The doll's bedstead was next taken, it was Minny's present to Mary. The sheets and pillow-cases were ruffled, and the quilt was embroidered with Mary's name, all done by Minny. Mary was much delighted with this, and all proceedings were stopped while she went to thank Minny and to bring her doll Estelle, who was immediately put to sleep, fine clothes and all. The next thing was the velocipede, which was sent to Henry by one of his uncles. Then there was a whispering between Henry and Mary, and the basket was take down and examined. "Here they are," said Henry, handing a heavy bundle to mamma and one to grandma, and a lighter one to papa.

"Our presents, you know," said Mary, "done by our ownselves."

These proved to be a very beautiful set of dessert plates, ornamented in Decalcomanie flowers for mamma, and another set in fruits for grandma.

"Now, I understand," said grandma; "and thank you, my dear children."

"What is the mystery?" asked papa.

"It is this," explained grandma; "those plates for Louise" (the name of their mother) "were done by these dear children at Burnside. Every day that they have been there this fall, they have spent several hours on them. They constantly asked my advice and opinion, but I found they did not follow it. I said I preferred fruits, and yet they put on flowers.

Now I understand, the flowers were for mamma, and these little wise children did not tell me anything about it.

" And," said mamma, " I had the same experience. I said I preferred flowers, but found the plates, which they ornamented here, were all done in fruits. You kept your secret thoroughly, dear children, and I am delighted with my flowery plates."

Henry and Mary were much pleased at their success, and jumped and danced about so much that papa had to call " Attention, Order," before he could open his package. It was more work of the same kind, being an ornamented portfolio. This all showed great industry for such merry little children, and I am afraid to tell you how much praise they had given them for their work.

The stereoscope was mamma's present to Henry. He had particularly wished for one which he could fill with his own pictures, such as steamboats, yachts, cars, and so on. Mary next found a beautiful Bohemian vase from

4

grandma to mamma, and a little box from papa to mamma which contained only a direction to look in the corner of the room, where a beautiful and convenient secretary, furnished with all varieties of writing materials, was labelled "Mamma," and a larger box, from papa and mamma to grandma, with the miniatures of Henry and Mary. They were taken together, Mary with her hat falling from her head as she stooped over some dear little yellow chickens, one of which Henry had in his hand, he being seated on the ground beside her. It was a very lovely picture, and the likenesses were perfect. Grandma could not have had anything she liked better. Mary's present from mamma was a set of electrical toys, and Henry's present from Minny was a knife with twenty-five blades. Then there was that lovely book, "The New Year's Bargain," from papa to Mary, and some other book for Henry.

"But, papa," said Henry, "you gave us

umbrellas, and don't you know the rule, only one present for each one ?"

" Oh," said papa, " I entirely forgot that, that is one of mamma's new rules which I am so old I cannot learn. The only way I can arrange is for me not to *give* you the books. I will put them on the table, and you can *take* them and not thank me ! How will that do mamma ?"

" We will let it go this time," said mamma, laughing, " but next Christmas I will be very particular."

There were many more presents of which I have not time to tell you, but after they were all examined, then all the thanking and kissing was done, and that is the end of this chapter.

V.

Which Tells the End of Christmas Day.

"EVERYTHING is done now," said Mary; "we must only have tea, a little play, and go to bed."

"Yes, dear, call Minny to put away the presents and the ruins of Dame Santaclaus. I am going to the library for a quiet hour before tea," said mamma.

"And I," said grandma, "want an hour's talk with papa, on some business affairs, so, if he can give me the time, we will go to his own little private room."

"And I," said Mary, "will help Minny."

Henry looked wistfully at his mother; "May I stay with you, mamma?" The permission was given, and the family party separated for a little while.

The lamps were not lighted in the library, but the wood fire cast its cheerful and fitful gleam over the room, dancing over its decorations, and revealing the subjects of the pictures, as it lighted up one and another of them.

Henry had drawn a large easy-chair to the fire for his mother, and seated himself on a low seat beside her. One of her hands was held in his, and, for a while, both were quiet. They were weary and glad to rest.

Presently Henry said : " Mamma, are you too tired to talk ?"

"No, my dear boy, was I ever too tired to talk to you ?"

" I never remember that you were too tired to do anything for either of us, my own precious, beautiful mamma."

Mrs. Montgomerie pressed the little hands that were holding hers, and then Henry said :

" Mamma, I have been wanting to ask you

something all day. Did you hear Minny's 'Glory Song,' this morning?"

"I did, dear, it wakened me, and I thought it was a lovely sound to hear as I began my Christmas day."

"But, mamma, how *could* Minny be so happy?"

"Why not, dear Henry, Minny is always happy, her trust and love keep her like a little child, no fear, and all joy!"

"But, mamma, don't you remember about her children?"

"Oh yes, dear, I had forgotten that they died on Christmas day, but Minny knows they are safe with their Saviour; why should she not sing a song of praise?"

"Oh, mamma! mamma! could you—would you *ever* be happy if I had gone away from you. Don't, don't say it. Mamma, ah, don't say you could do without me." Henry's tearful eyes and pleading tones said even more than his words.

Mrs. Montgomerie pressed him to her heart, how should she answer him?

"Tell me, mamma, tell me!" he urged.

"My boy, my precious boy, you're so dear to me, so a part of my very life, that I do not feel as if I ever could be happy again in the way that I am now, but I hope that I should have strength to praise Him who died, that you and I might live with Him forever. It would not be loving you less, my own dear boy, it would be a thanksgiving to Him who had taken you to Himself. The joy of your presence is so much to me that I cannot feel that there could ever be such happiness without you as I have now."

"Thank you, thank you, mamma. I hope I shall always be a joy to you."

Henry was silent for a time, and then again asked about Minny: "She was *really* happy; mamma, how could it be?"

"My dear, it was different with Minny. I cannot tell you all the circumstances, but Minny was so situated that her two children were to be separated from her, and she never expected to see them again. They were going

among strangers who might not be kind and
loving to them. While Minny was dreading
this, and praying to the Saviour to let her
keep her children, they were taken ill, and on
one bright Christmas morning He took them
where she had no fear for their happiness. It
was a relief to her to give them to Him, for
she knew He would carry the little ones in
His arms. I think Minny is happier on
Christmas than on any other day. She has
often told me that a peace came over her
when she knew that trouble and sorrow could
never touch her children again. It was a
different thing, dear Henry, from anything
that could happen to you ; we cannot compare
our feelings. Your loss to me now, would be
a sorrow that only the Saviour's loving hand
could enable me to bear."

" Mamma, dear, you know I should not want
you to be miserable, even then ; but, oh, I
hope we can always be together."

"I don't see how any one could be
so unkind as to take Minny's children

away. Was it before she came to live with us ?"

"Yes, dear, many years ago, but Minny never forgets it. She told me about it when she first came here to live. She thinks that her children are close beside the Saviour, and says, in her odd way of talking : 'Dey're all safe, Missus, de good Lord has dem all safe. He will be good to dem all de time.'"

"He will, wont He, mamma ?"

"Yes, my dear boy, and when Minny says, 'Thank the Lord,' she is thinking of her little ones."

"Poor Minny," said Henry, "I hope I shall always be kind and good to her."

They were thoughtful after this little conversation, and Henry laid his head upon his mother's hand in the peace of full content.

Soon in her lovely clear voice, mamma began to sing those beautiful Thanksgiving words in "The Children's Bread :"

> "Father, I would be bringing
> All grateful thanks to Thee :

My happy heart is singing
  A loving melody ;
And pleasant thoughts go ringing,
  Like sweet bells joyfully.

A thousand thanks I'm owing,
  For blessings Thou dost lend,
All day Thou art bestowing
  Love tokens without end ;
All night without my knowing
  They silently descend.

From all Thy works, Great Father,
  Something Thou dost receive :
Some fragrance Thou may'st gather,
  Some homage all can give :
My gratitude must rather
  In grateful loving live.

Thy little bird will sing Thee
  The blithest song he knows ;
Thy little flower will fling Thee
  The sweetest scent that blows :
Thy little child will bring Thee
  A heart that overflows."

Henry knew the words, and sang himself
into bright and cheerful thoughts again, and
as the hymn ceased, grandma and papa stood
behind them, listening to music that could
not be bought for money, but which rose

from hearts surrounded by love and hope and happiness.

Little Mary soon came in, lights and tea were brought, and, after tea, some short game was played by all together, and then the little ones, whose Christmas had been full of the joys of giving as well as of receiving, whose hearts were better for their quiet pleasures, went to rest and peaceful sleep.

The sleigh came for grandma ; she was carefully protected from the cold ; James and John were both on the box ; so that in the bright moonlight she had no fear of the long drive.

As she thanked her son and daughter for the pleasant hours she had passed with them, she said, in a low voice : " Henry, my son, thank God to-night for your wife and children."

Christmas day was over. Some of the glory which had heralded the first Christmas, had illumined the home at Brightside.

Peace, good-will to men !

VI.

About the New Doors.

THE next morning Henry and Mary were
wakened by a great hammering in the
hall near the nursery door.

"Henry, Henry, what can that be?" exclaimed Mary.

"I'll soon find out about it," said Henry,
with a very brave look, and he opened the
door, expecting to be obliged to defend the
house against an assault of very noisy and
determined robbers. To his great surprise, two
peaceful looking masons were breaking a hole
in the wall of mamma's dressing-room. The
hall carpet had been taken up, and other preparations made for them, so that Henry could
only ask what they were doing?

"We are to cut a door in this wall, Sir,

and another here," showing a place in the wall of Henry's dressing-room, said one of the masons; "but we are to wait till you are dressed."

" Thank you," said Henry, closing the door, to talk over with Mary this wonderful matter, for he did not think it right to question the masons, when his papa had not told him about it.

Mary thought it was "strawdinary" that new doors should be wanted in Christmas week.

"I believe there's something in it," said Henry, shaking his head very wisely; "and I will dress right off, so they can begin, for you see Mary, it will be much better for me to have a door into the hall, instead of having to come round through the nursery."

So Henry went to his room, and Mary began to dress. While they are so engaged I will tell you about these rooms. The nursery, where Henry and Mary had slept and played, for all the years of their young lives, was on

the south-east corner of the house. The east
windows opened upon a piazza, the roof of
which was high enough to permit the morning
sun to shine with its earliest beams into the
room ; many a lesson from its light and glory
had Minnie taught the children. I will tell
you what I mean about that some other time ;
now I want you to understand about the rooms.
Opposite to the east window, a door opened
into Henry's dressing-room. This room was
half the width of a large square hall, into
which the bedroom doors opened, and was on
the front of the house, having half of a large
window opening on a balcony, the other half
of the window was in mamma's dressing-room,
which was just like Henry's, only that it
opened into her room instead of into the
nursery.

The carpet of mamma's dressing-room had
been taken out, and the furniture removed, so
that the masons and carpenters could work.
Nothing had been said to the children about
it ; but as usual they were interested and de-

lighted, and hastened to be ready to watch the proceedings.

Minny soon came in, nodding her bright turban, and with her cheery, "Good-morning chil'n, did the noise wake you?"

"Oh yes, Minny, isn't it nice to hear such a pounding and hammering? Henry says it's like the taking of a fort."

Minny's laugh was pleasant to hear, and Henry soon came out, to explain and expound about the way the Bible warriors used to force their battering rams against the walls of cities, to make what they called a breach, and said that was what he meant, not a bombardment of a modern fort.

While they were talking, Minny said "Chil'n, look where de sunshine lies on de carpet. What does de brightness make you see dere?"

"The dust," said Mary. "The carpet looks quite clean everywhere else."

"Oh, but," said Henry, "don't look at the dust. Don't you see how much brighter the colors look in the sunshine; that's the best thing to see."

Minny's eyes brightened, the children had found the lesson she wished to teach them. "Now, dear chil'n, who is de light ob men?"

Both exclaimed, "Jesus," and repeated the text, she had taught them: "In Him was life, and the life was the light of men."

"When dis light, de blessed Lord," said Minny, "shines into your hearts, dear chil'n, He will bring to sight all de dust dat lies round in de holes, and de corners, and de dust dat lies on de good tings you do, and you will be sorry it was lying dere; and He will make all dat is bright in your hearts, brighter and more glorysome, shining it wid His own bright glory."

They were thoughtful as they looked at the broad line of light, revealing every thread of the carpet, and often, in after life, remembered Minny's lesson of *light as a revealer*.

"Now I know," said Henry, "what a verse

means in 'Who may abide the day of His coming?' —

> Christian, dost thou fear My coming,
> Are thy garments pure and white ;
> Wilt thou shrink before My shining,
> Dread the question of the light?

The ' question of the light,' must mean Christ shining in the heart. I know now, it is like asking if all is ready and clean. I read it to mamma one day, but did not know at all what it meant."

"Dat is it," said Minny. "I tink a room is clean and nice, den de sunshine comes in, and asks me, 'Did you sweep dis corner, I tink I see a little dust?' So bring de light ob Jesus in de heart, and you will soon see what keeps everything from being bright and shiny."

"Minny, how can I get the dust out?" asked Henry, in a low, earnest voice.

"Jesus de Lord is de refiner, and de purifier ob silver. His blood cleanseth from all unrighteousness. He will purge away de dross, if He shines in your hearts, my chil'n. It will be like de clear shining after de washing ob de rain. You must ask Him to do it for you. He is de only one who can make de hearts clean, wid no dust anywhere. He is de fountain for sin and uncleanness. Ask Him to shut de door ob your heart, on de side where de dust comes in, and to open de door to His light. If He will come and live in your hearts dere will be no dust," and then Minny began :

> "Sun of my soul ! Thou Saviour dear,
> It is not night if Thou be near ;
> Oh ! may no earth-born cloud arise
> To hide Thee from Thy servant's eyes.

> "Abide with me from morn till eve
> For without Thee I cannot live :
> Abide with me when night is nigh,
> For without Thee I dare not die."

The children sang with her as usual. Minny could not pronounce as they did, but the prayer arose from her heart with an earnestness that no words were needed to express.

The workmen stopped to listen to the singing, and though in the prayer that followed, they could only hear the murmur of voices, they waited until all was finished, before they resumed their labors.

" There they go again," said Henry. " I had forgotten all about the doors. Come, Mary, let us go to mamma and ask about them."

Mamma did not explain about the doors. She only told Henry to remove his books and clothes to a room on the other side of the nursery, until the alteration was completed. When he had done that, the furniture and carpet were taken out, and the workmen hammered and sawed, and planed, and painted for several days, before the doors were entirely .finished. There was a new door made between the dressing-rooms, and a door for each room into the hall. This hall was like a large square room, into which the bed-room doors opened. At one end was the staircase, and at the other, these important dressing-rooms, of which I shall tell you more when we come to New Year's day.

VII.

About the Little Dogs.

THE next morning after breakfast, Mary
thought the ruffles of the pillow cases on
the doll's bed ought to be fluted. Minny said
she would show her how to do it. Mary was
very quick in learning, and while she fluted
and Minny helped, Mary began as usual to ask
questions.

"Minny, what does 'extra' mean?"

"Why dat's an easy word," said Minny, with
her thoughts on laundry work; "it's de clothes
dat go in de wash besides de reg'lar number."

"Oh, Minny," said Mary, "that can't be,
because—"

Here Henry's voice was heard. "Mary,
Mary, Mary, come right down to the stable;

there's the duckiest little dogs down there I ever saw."

Down went the fluting iron, the pillow cases and the question were all forgotten, and Mary was soon running with Henry to the stable.

"Now, stop," said Henry ; "don't frighten them : they're Tan's little dogs, and Tan is afraid I'll hurt them : come up the stairs into the loft, they're in the room where Tom used to sleep." Tom was the coachman, and Tan was Tom's little dog.

They soon found the treasures. Fortunately Tan had gone out to take a walk, and they had an opportunity of, as Mary said, "zamining them." There were four, one white, he was the largest, one black, one curly brown, and one tan color, like a Scotch terrier.

"What funny little dogs," said Mary. "I like the white one the best, don't you?"

"Yes," said Henry, "he has such a brave look. Let's call him General."

"Oh, no," said Mary, "I think Carlo is a

great deal better : wont you, Henry, please, please call him Carlo."

"Certainly, my dear," replied Henry, trying to look like papa ; "just as you wish. He may not be a large dog, and then General would not be a very good name, so we will call him Carlo. And the others, what shall they be?"

"You name the black one, Henry, and I will name the brown—he shall be Dash—Carlo and Dash."

"The black one shall be Fido, and the tan one Dandy, he has such a way of putting his head on one side as if he thought he was handsome."

Just then a low growl was heard, and quickly putting the dogs down, they ran off from Tan's evident displeasure at their interference with her family. Nothing was thought of but the dogs, and the next day, as soon as breakfast was over, the children ran to the stable ; Tan having been seen to go out for her usual morning walk.

Calls of dismay were soon heard :

"Tom, Tom, where are the little dogs?
Oh, what have you done with them?"

"Sure and I've never touched them dogs,
it's herself has carried them off," said Tom.

"Oh, Tom, tell us, where *has* she taken
them?"

Tom came up into the hay loft, and pointed
to the children a place far out of reach, where
he supposed the dogs were, and then showed
them a small opening in the mound of hay,
through which he asserted Tan had carried
the dogs. After their first visit, he said, Tan
had seemed much troubled. She had then
worked a passage through the hay, and taken
them one by one into it. It was so small that
no one could reach her little dogs but
herself.

The children put their arms in as far as
possible, but could not find any trace of them,
and there was nothing to do but to wait till
Carlo and Dash, Fido, and Dandy would work
their own way out. Tom promised to let
them know as soon as he found them. And

the children returned home much disappointed. As they went home, Mary asked,

"Oh, Henry, do tell me what an 'extra' is?"

"An extra," said Henry, "it's a railroad train that comes besides the regular ones—there's mamma calling, I wonder what is going to happen?"

The children were always ready to find some new source of interest or amusement, and went into great raptures when mamma told them they were to go on Friday afternoon to stay with grandma till Monday. They had often passed one day at Burnside, but this was a visit, and was like a journey, requiring trunks and so on. Mary had no bounds to her joy, until the idea of parting with papa and mamma was thought of.

"Oh, Henry," said she, "it's bad about not kissing papa and mamma at night."

"Yes," Henry said, "that is bad, but I'll tell you what we'll do, we will have four kisses before we go, that will be one for each night and one to spare."

Mary laughed at "one to spare," and said she never had any to spare.

"You needn't take a fellow up so," said Henry, whose love for his mother was intense; "you know what I mean."

"Yes, dear," said Mary, kissing him, "don't be angry. We'll kiss and kiss and have all we can."

The preparations began at once, and soon two little valises were packed, with everything needful for Friday night, and Saturday and Sunday. They were to return on Monday. Just before the sleigh came to the door, Mary whispered that they had better bid the pony and the cow good-bye, and at the same time they could see once more about the little dogs. So they ran to the stable, but could find no trace of the new favorites. They told Frolic, the pony, about their going, to which information he whinnied his reply. Then Susie the cow heard all about it, but said nothing in return, which made Henry say :

"I think Susie is stupid and rude. Did you see how Frolic looked after us—he knows all I say."

"I don't think Susie would be rude if she knew any better," said Mary, who made excuses for everything.

"But," replied Henry, "it is her duty to know better—papa always says so. Don't you remember Mary, the day I said I did not know about answering that lady, papa said it was no excuse, I ought to have known."

Mary considered the matter gravely as they walked home, and as she entered the door, had decided, "Cows are not people," which she said in a voice so determined and loud, that her father and mother, who were standing on the piazza, both laughed, and papa exclaimed : "What a wise little girl ! have you just made that discovery, my little daughter ?"

"Oh dear !" said Mary, "I didn't mean to say that so loud, it belonged to something before, don't ask me about it."

"Certainly not, my birdie ; mamma and I

will not trouble you to say why you think
so. You are quite right, so now say Good-
bye."

The number of kisses given and taken and
laid up in store for nights was something
wonderful, and their bright faces, together with
Minny's, whose joy always illumined her whole
countenance, made the sleigh look as if Happiness was going off on a frolic.

"What had Mary been thinking of?" asked
Mr. Montgomerie of his wife, after the children
had gone.

"I cannot imagine," she replied, "unless
the animals failed to reply to her Good-byes.
I am sometimes afraid Mary thinks too
much."

"There is no danger dear, for either of our
children, while they play so heartily. Thinking will not harm such vigorous natures. I
always want Mary to be satisfied when she
tries to find out anything, but I did not ask
her what brought about her comical conclusion. As the conclusion was correct, the road

by which she reached it need not be re-
traced."

They went in and closed the door, and
Brightside seemed still and lonely during the
absence of the little ones.

VIII.

About Burnside.

AN hour's merry drive in the sleigh, and grandmamma's beautiful home was reached. Grandmamma's little dog barked his welcome as the sleigh approached ; grandmamma's parrot from the hall, as the door opened, called, "Come in, come in, cold day," and dear grandmamma herself helped them out of the sleigh, kissing their cold but rosy cheeks, and telling how glad she was to see them, while John took charge of Minny and the valises.

In rather a magnificent way Henry said, "That is right John, take in our luggage."

John replied respectfully, " All right Mas'r, I'll see eberyting is all safe."

The parrot kept on "All right, all safe, come in, shut the door, all right, poor Polly."

"Poor Polly," said Mary laughing; "I think you're a very rich Polly; you have the best time any old bird ever had."

Polly at this remark put her head on one side, sharpened her bill, and called: "Grandma come in, Polly wants supper, poor Polly."

"Oh, you funny Polly," said Mary; "you've got everything you want, but you shall have your supper when we do, can't she grandma?"

"Yes, dear, to be sure she shall. Now run up stairs to the rooms next to mine, and prepare for tea, it will be ready in a few minutes."

Polly had required so much attention that Jip, the dog, felt himself greatly neglected, and showed his determination to be noticed by jumping on Henry and Mary, and by barking and demonstrating his pleasure in the usual manner of little dogs.

"Come little black doggy," said Henry, "come with us to get ready."

They all scrambled up together, for Jip was always in the way, and tried to get up one stair ahead, and then to turn round to see if they were coming, and then to squeeze in between them, so that he could have all their attention. He ought to have been contented, and, perhaps, might have been, but, unfortunately for him, Polly called out, "Everybody all gone! Poor Polly! S'cat Jip, s'cat!" Now Jip very much disliked to have Polly say "S'cat" to him, so he turned round so suddenly, to bark at Polly, that he tripped Mary, who fell against Henry, and he only saved himself and her by seizing the baluster and falling on Jip. There was a general upset, and Jip crawled out from under Henry a very much mortified dog. If I were to tell you how many odd things Polly called out to them, or all that Jip did, or how lovely the two little rooms were which grandma had prepared for them, and how Minny had opened the valises, and how much she had to say, I am afraid this chapter would be so long that you would be tired. So you must imagine all this, and go down with them to the dining-room, where grandma was waiting.

They were soon seated, grandma at the head of the little table, with her bright silver urn and tea service before her. Henry opposite, all ready to help to the chicken croquettes, so brown and nice, Mary at one side, with the plate of biscuit in front of her, and Polly the other side, gravely watching all that was done. Polly's custom was to walk round from plate to plate, talking, and sometimes, I am sorry to say, helping herself. Grandma asked a blessing on their food, and Polly very properly bowed her head, and drooped her wings, until it was over; then she very irreverently exclaimed, " That's done, hurry up." Henry and Mary screamed with laughter, and John, the most dignified of waiters, seemed to be choking behind his silver tray, which he held up before his face.

" Oh, naughty Polly," said grandma, " will you never learn to be polite ?"—" Poor Polly

so hungry," was the reply, and then Polly
took a nibble out of the top of Mary's biscuit.
The biscuits were in the shape of little towers,
and Mary had placed one by her plate. "Oh,
Polly, what are you doing!" exclaimed Mary.
Polly said, "Don't eat so much, my dear,"
and then walked up to the sugar bowl. It
was found best for the peace of all parties, to
help Polly first, after which, the various good
things, that no one ever had as nice as grandma, were fully enjoyed.

"Henry," said grandma, "did your mother
say you could stay until Monday?"

"Yes, grandma, the sleigh is to come for
us at ten o'clock. Are you going home with us
for New Year's day?"

"No, my dear boy, I have a dinner on that
day for my class in the Mission Church, so
that I must let you go home without me."

"Oh, grandma, I am so sorry, for I think
something is going to happen. There have
been so many doors cut, that I think they
mean something."

6

"Come in, come in," said Polly.

"Polly always says 'come in,' when she hears of doors," said grandma; "you must find out the meaning of the doors first, and I will try to drive over on Tuesday and hear about it. When do you recommence your lessons?"

"Not until Wednesday, and we are to take French lessons from the blind lady who boards in the village."

"Grandma," said Mary, "*must* we have so much business talk. This is a journey, you know."

"A journey where, dear?" asked grandma.

"Why, grandma, you know we brought little trunks—we are travelling."

"Oh yes," said grandma, "I understand—I hope you find your rooms comfortable, Miss Montgomerie. Is your maid with you, or do you require one of the housemaids?"

"Oh, grandma, how funny you are. I am very comfortable, thank you ma'am, my maid is with me. Our rooms are very cheerful, you have a very nice hotel, ma'am."

"I am very glad you like it, Miss Montgomerie. Are you going to take a long journey?" replied grandma.

"Not very long, ma'am, we must return home on Monday. Don't you think so, Mr. Montgomerie?"

"Yes, my dear," said Henry, "my business will oblige me to return."

"Do you wish hot water in the morning to shave, sir?" asked grandma, very gravely.

"Oh, grandma, grandma," exclaimed Henry, laughing, "I don't believe I can be a gentleman, I'm your little boy."

"Poor boy," said Polly, "go to bed."

"Oh, Polly, you impolite bird, be quiet, we are talking to grandma," said Mary, but Polly had been left out long enough, and she insisted on being attended to.

"Polly you cannot come to the table any more if you give so much trouble. I hope, Miss Montgomerie, my parrot does not annoy you," said grandma.

" Oh, no, ma'am, I think she is lovely. May I take her to her cage ?"

Polly at once perched herself on Mary's shoulder, singing, " Pretty Poll, pretty Poll, you're a jolly old doll, pretty Poll, pretty Poll." Mary took her to her cage in the hall, where she soon went to sleep. Then Henry and Mary superintended Jip's going to bed, kissed him good-night, and ran to the parlor, where Mary jumped on grandma's lap, quite forgetting about the journey, and putting her arms round her neck, asked for a story.

" Oh, do," said Henry, bringing his chair close beside Mrs. Montgomerie, " tell us about animals."

Mrs. Montgomerie told them the following story, which she had read in one of the periodicals :

" A gentleman had a pet cat, which lived chiefly in his library. One day he brought a parrot home, and had it on a standing perch. While he was talking to it and playing with it, pussy was watching from under the sofa with jealous eyes. Presently her master went out, and Polly began to settle her feathers. Pussy found out the new comer was a bird, 'and a very good bird for eating, no doubt,' she said. She crept out a little from under the sofa, 'a chicken, a green chicken, I will see about it.' Polly then first discovered her, and in horror climbed to the top perch. 'A chicken, yes, a green chicken,' repeated pussy preparing for a spring. Polly's alarm knew no bounds, and as pussy approached, in despair at her danger, screamed, 'Jack, Jack, have you had your breakfast ?' Pussy jumped back. 'It's a gentleman ! what a dreadful mistake, a gentleman, and not a chicken at all.'"

The children laughed heartily, then Mary said, thoughtfully : "Do you think the cat really thought that, grandma ?"

"No, dear, I do not, but I think that the cat was much surprised and frightened, and knew there was something strange about it."

"But you believe animals think, don't you, grandma ?" asked Henry.

" Certainly, I do. Jip thinks, when he stops at a corner to see which way I will turn ; pussy thinks, when she hides her kittens ; Polly thinks, when she teases Jip and then laughs at him."

" Oh, grandma, did you teach her to put her head down when you ask a blessing !"

" No, dear, she only imitates our doing so. I do not think she is quite as sensible as her talking makes her seem, but she thinks sometimes."

" I don't like that story so much if the cat did not really think that. I think it's wrong," said Mary.

" No, Mary," replied Henry, " it's figurative."

" What do you mean ? Do you mean anything about arithmetic ?" asked Mary.

" No, indeed, I mean what papa told me, that in stories when they make believe that animals and trees and such things talk and think, it is figurative, that is," and Henry stopped to think ; " that is—it is like a picture of something, only in your thoughts, instead

of your seeing it—oh, grandma, do tell Mary.
I don't know how to explain it."

"I do not wonder at that, dear Henry, it is
not easy to explain, but you can understand
what is called an illustration or an example.
If I say a door to a house, it is something
real, and you know what I mean. If I say a
door to your heart, it is figurative. I am talking
of something you cannot see, and explaining
it by speaking of it as of something which you
can see and understand."

"Minny told me to keep the door of my
heart open on the side where the light of
Jesus would come in. I understood her ; was
it figurative ?" replied Henry.

"Yes, dear, it was. Figurative language is
the use of words in a different meaning from
the one we are accustomed to. When in the
story of the cat, she is spoken of exactly as
if she understood, and thought, and talked, it
is a kind of figurative writing. There are
several kinds, but I think you know enough
about it for such a little boy,"

"Thank you, dear grandma, but sometimes it is real fun to tell about how animals think. I don't know about that cat, but little Tan thought a great deal. She did a wonderful thing. She was afraid we would hurt her little dogs, and she hid them in the hay, so far off that we could not get to them, and then made a little way through the hay, just large enough for her to go through. Tom said it was ten feet at least from where she hid the dogs."

"Papa called it a 'terraynean passage," said Mary, very gravely.

"I think he must have said *subterranean* —which means, really, under or through the earth," said grandma. "He was talking figuratively, for this was through the hay," said grandma.

"That figgertive is very hard. I'm going to believe all about it, and not worry to understand," answered Mary.

"Do so, dear Mary. When your papa and mamma tell you anything, you are safe in believing it, and right to wait until you have enough knowledge to help you to understand it."

"Yes," said Mary, "when papa, and mamma, and you, and Bible, and Minny, and Henry tell me a thing, I always know it is so. Why do I?"

"Because you have confidence in them, dear; you are sure they will not deceive you. You know they are true. That's the way Job felt, when he said: 'I know in whom I have believed.'"

"Grandma, I love to feel sure, it's like standing on a rock," said Henry.

"The rain descended, and the floods came and beat upon that house, and it fell not, for it was founded upon a rock," said grandma.

"You are all talking figgerative again, *don't*," said Mary.

"Mary dear," replied grandma, "say figurative, very plainly."

Mary did so.

"Now say subterranean and comfortable."

Mary looked rather uncomfortable, but pronounced the words correctly.

" Now, dear, I want you and Henry to give me four reasons, why our Saviour is figuratively called a rock."

" Because He is so firm," said Henry. " We can be so sure of Him."

" You mean He is so true in all He says and promises, do you not?" asked grandma.

" Yes, grandma, and He is a shelter, like a rock. And you know, grandma, the rock makes a shadow too."

" Yes indeed, replied grandma. Do you remember, in Miss Warner's story, about Ellen. She says of her, 'She found the great Rock in the weary land, and lay down in the shadow of it.' I may not have the exact words, but that is the idea."

Oh, grandma," said Mary, " I remember that, and she has your name too."

" Yes," said grandma, " perhaps that is one reason I always loved her so. Now we have two reasons, a rock is *firm*, and a *shelter*."

"Grandma, they make the lower parts of houses out of rocks ; they stand on them," said Mary.

" Yes," said grandma, "a foundation, now one more."

" Didn't the water for the Israelites come out of a rock, grandma ?" asked Henry. " It kept them alive you know."

" That will do. Now remember Christ Jesus is figuratively a rock, because He has the qualities of a rock, firmness, power to shelter, power to uphold whatever rests upon Him ; and as the rock of the desert gave water to support life, so does He give us living water, which supports our spiritual life."

" Grandma dear, it's getting to be a little like school," said Mary.

" Run and hide then," said grandma ; " quick now. Henry and I will find you."

Mary was off in a minute, and a loud "whoop" from the hall, told that she was hidden.

"Where can she be !" said grandma. " I don't see her anywhere."

Polly waked up, and in a sleepy tone, said : " Go to bed, go to bed, s'cat."

At this Mary laughed, and so they found her in a little closet under the stairs. " That was Polly's fault," said Mary.

" Whoop," cried Henry.

" Why, that sounded close by us. Where can he be, there is nothing here to hide in ?" said grandma.

They looked everywhere, Polly still sleepily entreating them to go to bed ; but at last they found him behind an overcoat, which was hanging on the hat stand. That was a capital place, and then grandma hid. She was found behind the bay-window curtains. Once more round, and then they said " Goodnight." It was nearly a half hour after their usual time, and as travellers, they ought to go to bed early.

The little brown heads were laid to rest, but they were not ready to sleep.

" Henry, Henry, are you awake ?" called Mary to him.

"Yes, dear, a little awake."

"Don't you think it is very dark? I like to have a light."

"I don't care for it. You surely are not afraid."

"Oh, no, not at all, only I don't know zactly what is coming. I think a light is more 'greeable."

"It is, in the day time. I don't think it would be dark at night, unless it was best for us. If it was day all the time, we should want to play without stopping."

"We could go to sleep in the shadow of a rock, you know, Henry."

"Yes, dear, but we need night now. You know in that other world, we shall not have any night."

"After we die, you mean. That will be very nice. Do you think there will be any shade, or all sunshine?"

"Mary dear, the Bible speaks of the tree of Paradise, so there may be shade; but don't you remember what mamma told us about a different light in that world, from the sunshine here. And we shall be changed too, perhaps we shall not want shade then."

"Henry, I don't believe I want to think about it any more. Good-night."

"Chil'n," said Minny, putting her head in the door; "I don't 'spect it's good for you to talk any more; better go to sleep. You have talked so much, you have no sleep in your little heads."

"Nor in my little feet either," said Mary. "I want to get up, and run everywhere."

"Dat will neber do," said Minny. "I'll leave the door open, and sing to you; now try to go to sleep."

So Minny sat with her work in the hall singing in a soft, low voice, which soon soothed the little ones to rest:

> In de land, of 'no night,'
> 'Twill be beautiful light,
>   For Jesus is dere.
>
> Light, soft and glorious,
> Jesus victorious,
>   Light eberywhere.

'Tis de Saviour's own shining,
'Tis de cloud's silver lining,
'Tis Jesus my light.

They heard no more, but Minny repeated over and over again : "Jesus *my* light." Jesus was, indeed, the light and the life of this His earnest follower. Minny's Christian life, her daily path, was illumined in a way that seemed wonderful to those who knew her. She never seemed to have dark or dreary days ; her secret was a simple one. She walked in the light.

Mrs. Montgomerie came up with her candle to go to her room. " Are the children asleep, Minny ?" she asked.

" Yes, Mis' Gomerie. I hope I didn't 'sturb you with singing to them. They seemed kinder 'cited, and couldn't sleep, so I just sang them right off. Please come in, and see how lovely and peaceful dey is. May de good Lord bless dem chil'n."

Mrs. Montgomerie looked at the bright

healthful faces of her little ones, whom she loved so dearly, and gave an earnest response to Minny's prayer.

Soon all were at rest in Burnside.

IX.

About Saturday and Sorella.

THE children slept late the next morning. Mary was awakened by a scratching at the door.

"I do believe that is Jip," she exclaimed, and opening the door, found the little dog had come in search of his playmates. "Come in, little black doggie, run in that other room and call Henry." Jip understood, and with one bound on Henry's bed, waked him.

"Hallo, old fellow! what do you mean by such performances?" Jip jumped on the bed, and they were pretty soon having a good frolic together, and Jip's performances were quite equalled by Henry's. It was a long time before they were ready for breakfast. At last they went down, and had to ask

7

grandma to excuse them for being late. She
did not seem to care about it, and they all
had a very happy breakfast. Polly walked
about the table, and said a great many very
amusing things. After breakfast, while grandma was occupied, the children played with
Jip, and talked with Polly; then they were
delighted to have a fine frolic of snow-balling.
Grandma sat in the sunshine, on the south
piazza, while the children played. They
snow-balled Jip, and for a while he thought
it was great fun, but at last he was tired, and
just as Henry had raised his hand to throw
one more, Jip was gone. "Where did Jip
go," exclaimed Henry ; " he was here just this
minute. He has not gone off on the lawn, for
I would see him on the snow. Where can he
be ?"

Grandma laughed, and said : "Look for him.
I know where he is." They looked everywhere, under the dried bushes, round the
house, on the piazza, but no Jip. Suddenly
Mary discovered the tip of a brown nose

coming out from under Grandma's dress, where Jip had hidden, and where, if he had not wanted to watch the children, they would not have found him. The discovery was followed by such a sudden snowball right on his little nose, that Jip scrambled out and ran off down the carriage-path to the stable. The children followed, and as grandma knew that they would have enough to amuse them there, she went in the house to read.

After a long time, Mary came back, alone, and said Henry was sliding down hill, and she preferred to come in, as she was cold. Grandma took her on her lap, took off her wrappings and cold boots, sent for some hot soup for lunch, so that soon she was warm again, and ready for a nice talk. She began the conversation herself, for she said she " had something saved up to ask grandma."

Grandma was rather surprised when she heard what it was. I will tell you the conversation.

" Grandma, am I very beautiful ?" asked Mary.

"Yes, dear," replied grandma; "why do you ask?"

"Some one told me so, and I went up to my glass and looked. Don't you think it's nice to be beautiful?" asked Mary, as grandma did not say anything more.

"Yes, dear, very," said grandma.

"I'm glad I am," said Mary.

"So am I," said grandma; "but suppose you were to fall off my lap, with your face in the fire, and be burned, you would not be beautiful any more, or if you were to fall down stairs and break your nose."

"Oh, grandma!" exclaimed Mary, "couldn't anything be done?"

"I am afraid we could not make you beautiful again."

"Would you love me, grandma?"

"Just as much as I do now, dear. I do not love you because you are beautiful."

"But it helps, don't it, grandma?"

"It is very pleasant to me, dear, and our heavenly Father has shown His love to us by surrounding us with much that is beautiful ; you love to see how beautiful your dear mamma is, and yet you would love her just as well if her face were pale, and her hair gray. You love something in her which is better than her beauty, something that neither accident nor time can destroy."

" I think I know what you mean, grandma. I love mamma's self, because she is good and kind, and, oh dear, because she *is* mamma."

" Yes, dear, and I love you because you are my own little Mary, and because you are kind and true, and try to make every one and everything happy, and because you love me, and because you are one of the little lambs of Christ's flock ; you would have all these loveable qualities, if you were to lose your beauty, and no fall in the fire or down-stairs would take them away. So I want you to think more of preserving the beauty of your character than of your face."

" Grandma," said Mary, after a long pause, " can't anything be done with it ?"

" With what, dear ?"

" With my face, grandma." Mary did not
venture to say " beautiful face."

" Do you mean, can you make your beauty
useful ?"

" Yes, grandma, I mean, can I do anything
good with it ?"

" I think, dear, all beauty helps to make us
enjoy life, just as beautiful flowers do, and I
think you had better do just what they do,
and omit what they omit."

" Oh, you funny grandma ! I don't believe
flowers think about themselves at all."

" That is exactly what I mean, they do not
think at all about their beauty, they do not
try to display it, nor try to increase it, nor do
they turn to show it to the passers-by. This
is what they do *not* do.

" What they *do*, is to be bright and cheerful,
to hang on their little stems just where they
grow, or if duty calls them, to go willingly
to brighten up some sick room, or dark parlor,
or gay party, or to help to make some one

beautiful or happy. They live their little lives in the service of others, if they are needed ; if not, they live quietly on their stems, or hidden in some little nook. Minny would tell you of one other thing that they do. They try to keep in the *light*. They push their little heads from under the leaves to feel the bright warm rays of the sun. Now, dear little girl, why do flowers do this ? they do not think."

" Grandma, I think they're made so, it's the inside that makes them do so."

" Do you mean it's their nature, my dear ?"

" Yes, grandma, you know they must do so."

" Now, dear Mary, remember this as well as the rest I have told you. If it is in your heart to do right, you will do so. Ask your Saviour to help you to keep your little heart right, and your hands, and feet, and face too, will be directed how to serve Him."

" And, grandma, Minny says, let the Saviour's light shine into my heart. I know how she means, don't you ?"

"Yes, dear, I know, and I trust He will ever be your Guiding Light. Now we have talked enough, and I want you to do what the little four-o'clock flowers do."

"What is that grandma?"

"They shut their little eyes and seem to go to sleep—even when it is bright light."

"Yes, dear grandma, I will, for I was awake a long time last night, and then what may we do after dinner?"

"After dinner I am going to have Sorella and Jocko here, to play with you. Now have a nice little sleep, for Jocko will want all your attention."

Mary was too delighted to say anything but, "You dear, darling grandma. I'd rather have Sorella and Jocko than the Queen of England," and off she ran to tell Minny.and to take her nap.

Soon after dinner the jingling sleigh bells told them that Sorella and Jocko had come, and Polly's screams of "Come in, come in," and then her "Hallo, hallo, hallo," were very

comical, particularly if you could have seen
her look of surprise at Jocko. She stood with
one foot to her ear as if thinking about this
new arrival, saying, " Hallo" in rather a subdued voice, as if Jocko might be somebody
whom she had better not offend.

Sorella was an odd looking child, not quite
as old as Henry in years, but much older in
her ways and thoughts. She had a dark skin,
but lighter in some places than others ; the
end of her nose, and the tips of her fingers
were quite white, then her hair was partly
reddish black, her eyes and teeth were very
fine, and she had a quiet happy face ; but still
she was more odd than pretty. Jocko, who
rarely left her, was not a common monkey.
He was very small, of a mouse color, with a
white face and a head that looked like a lord
chancellor's wig, only mouse color. Instead
of his body being rough and hairy, his hair
was thick and soft like fur. A very clean and
nice playfellow, and very bright and intelli-
gent. He had on his blue ribbon and bell,

which, when Polly heard, she said, "Scat," but very softly and rather politely. Jocko took no notice of her, but he was rather afraid of Jip, and to Jip's great astonishment he ran up the curtain of the window, and sat on the cornice making such comical faces that the children shouted with laughter. The afternoon passed very happily. Sorella did not know many plays, but with grandma's help she soon learned, and played and talked as merrily as any of them. Jocko behaved very well, but rather preferred the cornice to Sorella's shoulder. The time passed very quickly, and they had an early tea, so that Sorella could go home by eight o'clock. Polly would not come to the table, but when she wanted anything called, "Mary, come here, Polly wants cake." Mary was quite fatigued with waiting on Polly, and attending to Jocko, who took a great fancy to her, and by the time they were gone was quite ready to go to bed.

When Sorella said Good-bye, she said to Mrs. Montgomerie :

"I thank you, madame, for your goodness to me. Grandfather says he hopes I can return your kindness some day."

Grandma kissed her Good-by, but thought it was an odd sort of speech to make, and she and Henry talked about it after sleepy little Mary had gone to bed.

Henry told his grandmamma all about the various pleasures of the day ; asked her advice about the cottage on the island, which he hoped to begin to build in the spring ; decided about the bridge from the mainland to the island, that it had better be two planks wide and have a railing, and that he had no objections to James building it, if he could do the cottage himself. When this was all planned he bade his dear, kind grandma good-night, and went softly to his room lest he should waken Mary.

X.

Sunday.

SO many little children think that Sunday is a very tiresome day. I will tell you exactly how Henry and Mary enjoyed it.

When they dressed in the morning they talked very pleasantly together, but more about how they should pass the day, than about other things. After their prayers Minny said, "Dis is de day de Lord hath made," and the children answered, "Let us be glad and rejoice in it." She then began the morning hymn :

> " Welcome sweet day of rest,
>   That saw the Lord arise ;
>   Welcome to this reviving breast,
>   And these rejoicing eyes."

Their young voices followed that of their

good Minny, making sweet melody on this
Sabbath morning. When the hymn was
finished they went to breakfast, which was
always a little earlier on Sunday than on
other days. They had a happy talk with
grandma, then the sleigh came to the door,
and though it was very early, they were ready
to go as soon as grandma was. She wanted
to stop before going to church to see two
persons who were ill. One was Nora Herndon, the little girl who had been hurt at the
mill, and who was now only able to sit up.
Grandma had a bright, happy book, which she
let Mary take to her. She was supported by
pillows, and looked very comfortable in her
blue flannel sacque which Mary's mother had
sent to her on Christmas; and she was glad
to have an opportunity to thank Mary for the
doll and the picture which she had sent at the
same time.

The book from grandma "came," as she
said, "just at the right time," and in answer
to Mary's expression of sorrow at her being

obliged to remain so long in bed, she said,
"Oh, I don't mind it, now that the pain is
better. Every one is so kind to me, and the
bright, warm sun comes in the window,
and seems to do me good. Minny says it has
'healing in its wings.' I shall soon be well
again, then I mean to give thanks in the
Lord's house."

Mary told grandma how happy Nora was,
and grandma said she was "a good little girl."

"Is she one of the lambs?" said Mary.

"Yes, dear, she truly is, and she tries to
keep near to the Shepherd."

After this they stopped to see another sick
person, who was too weak to hold a book.
Grandma had brought to her one of those
sets of Bible verses in large print, which could
be hung where she could read them, without
the fatigue of holding a book. She was very
grateful, and said it was like talking to the
Shepherd, to read about the "green pastures
and still waters," and then to say, "I will fear
no evil." Mrs. Montgomerie told her that

every Christian could dwell in green pastures
if they would keep near the fountain of
Christ's love. The sick woman answered in
the words of a hymn :

> "Prone to wander, Lord, I feel it,
> Prone to leave the Lord I love ;
> Here's my heart, oh ! take it, keep it,
> Keep it for Thy courts above."

The little bell of the Mission chapel was
ringing, and Mrs. Montgomerie was obliged
to go.

"Come, grandma," said Mary, "I'm so
afraid we shall be late, and I want to hear the
children sing before the service."

"You shall hear them, my dear child.
They sing first, to-day, the opening verses of
the service. Our little chapel, you know, is
different from the church you attend. We
have no regular choir or organ. Eight of the
Sunday-school children lead the music. It is
very nice music, and I am sure you will like it."

They did like it very much, when they were
nicely seated in grandma's pew and the

service began. This Mission Chapel was built for the use of a large number of factory people who lived near the village. The church, which was the other side, nearly a mile from the village, was too far for the work-people, and on their account this little chapel had been erected. The Rev. Mr. Clark preached every afternoon in the chapel, but in the morning, if there was no clergyman who could come, the superintendent of the Sunday-school read the service, and after it a half hour was passed in singing. The morning services were on this day conducted by Mr. Wordin, the superintendent. The eight children sang two of the sentences before the service, and led the responses. They were very much interested in their duties, and as Mrs. Montgomerie instructed them in the proper reading of God's holy word, they responded in a solemn and yet animated tone. In whatever any of the Montgomerie family were interested, there was at once infused an element of joy. They believed that our Lord had not repealed the joyfulness of the Israelitish worship. "Thou shalt keep the feast, and thou shalt rejoice before the Lord thy God." "Thou shalt rejoice in the feast, thou and thy son and thy daughter, and thy man-servant and thy maid-servant, and the Levite, the stranger, and the fatherless, and the widow, that are within thy gates." (Deut. xvi.)

"The Gospel is good tidings of *great joy*," Mrs. Montgomerie would remind her friends. And as joyful people, like sunshine, brighten all their surroundings, so even the chapel had a brighter, happier mode of worship from Mrs. Montgomerie's influence. Nothing was dreary. The music and responses went, as Henry said, "right up."

After the service, Mr Wordin came down from the desk, and said, "We will continue to praise and to worship God by singing the 109th selection, beginning—

"'O praise the Lord with one consent.'"

After this Mr. Wordin said, "If any of the children have any favorite hymn which they

8

wish sung, they can bring the number to me, written on a piece of paper, as I explained last Sunday."

Four pieces of paper were handed to him. On the first was Hymn Fifty-third, on the subject of Isaiah, Chapter Sixtieth. Mr. Wordin said a few words explanatory of the subject of the chapter, after which the hymn was sung. On the next paper was written Hymn Eighty-fourth. On this he explained the influence of the seasons in bringing forth the fruits of the earth, and how even the cold snow protected and fertilized the ground. The next hymn chosen was the one hundred and fiftieth. On reading this number, Mr. Wordin told them the "Old, old story" of Christ's redeeming love. "A story old as creation," he said ; "a redemption ready for the first sinner. As soon as there was a sinner, there was a Saviour. And it has not changed since then, a Saviour for every sinner ! No sin so dark or heavy that He cannot blot it out, no sinner so despairing that He cannot turn his tears and sorrows to praises and joy."

There was not a voice in the chapel that did not join in the outburst of praise from a soul redeemed.

> "Lord with glowing heart I'd praise Thee,
>   For the bliss Thy love bestows ;
>   For the pardoning grace that saves me,
>   ·And the peace that from it flows."

The last hymn given, was the beautiful prayer for guidance, Number one hundred and seventy-seven.

Mr. Wordin read it, and then compared the journey of the Israelites with the Christian life. He particularly spoke of the Guiding Cloud, and told how, on each morning, the Israelites looked from their tent doors to the centre of the encampment, where the Tabernacle was erected, and over which rested the Cloud of bright glory—the symbol of Jehovah's presence. If it were stationary, standing like a pillar, between earth and heaven, they knew that they were not to move that day. Then they prepared to take part in the morning sacrifice, and went out to gather manna for their morning meal, sure that the Lord had sent them their daily bread, and that He watched and guarded. But if, as they looked, the cloud slowly rose towards the clear blue sky, and then floated off towards the front of the encampment, all was haste and preparation to follow it. Each family obeyed the movement of the cloud, and then stood ready for the journey onward.

On the first sound of the silver trumpets, the camp on the eastern side went forward, and on the second sounding, the camp on the southern side, and so on all in order, just as the Lord had directed Moses, they followed the cloud. At the commandment of the Lord they rested in their tents, and at the commandment of the Lord they journeyed— "when the cloud abode from even unto the morning, and that the cloud was taken up in the morning, then they journeyed." "So my dear friends," said he, "let us follow Christ our Jehovah, praying to Him in the words chosen for us—

"'Guide me, O Thou great Jehovah.'"

Every heart seemed impressed, and after Mr. Wordin pronounced the words of St. Paul to the Philippians—"Now unto God our Father, be glory for ever and ever. Amen"— they all quietly left the chapel.

There was no talking or laughing. The prayer for guidance rested upon them in quietness and peace. When Mrs. Montgomerie and the children were seated in the carriage, Henry said :

" Grandma, that is the loveliest little church I ever went to. It's so nice to feel that you help. I like to sing and pray with all the rest. Don't you, Mary ?"

" Yes, indeed, I do, and it was beautiful to think about the people going out and looking at the cloud. Who were those people, grandma ?"

" The Israelites, my dear. I will tell you about them when we go home."

" Grandma," said Henry, "*I* know about them, and I think it was a so much nicer thing to do, than to be looking out in the morning to see if it will rain. They looked at a *bright* cloud, didn't they, grandma ?"

And with such pleasant conversation the drive was soon over. The wagon with the servants, who had also all been to church, followed down the carriage road ; for Mrs. Montgomerie rejoiced with *all* who were within her gates, men-servants and maid-servants.

On their return, grandma gave the children picture puzzles, like dissecting maps, to put together. One was Daniel and the Lions, another was the History of Elijah. They occupied themselves quietly with these while grandma had an hour in her room.

At one o'clock there was a nice lunch, and at two o'clock the carriage came again to take grandma to the afternoon service. The children remained at home with Minny. They played church, Henry being the clergyman, and Mary and Minny the congregation. Henry preached a very good sermon about the bright cloud, to which his congregation listened very attentively; it was rather short, and so he filled up the time with singing. After this they put on their snow-boots and walked a long way down the road, to meet grandma. James saw them coming, and stopped to take them in. "Dear little bright-eyed snow birds," grandma said, as they jumped in beside her. Minny walked back, her turban nodding about as she sang some improvised song of praise. Mary exclaimed: "I'm just as happy as I can be, I don't believe the little Israel children had half as nice a time."

Grandma said, "Every child had its own dear mother and father, and home, but it is probable you have the easiest life."

"I should have liked getting the little white balls of manna, grandma, wouldn't you?"

Grandma thought she should have liked that very much, and by that time they were at home, and Jip and Polly showing, in their way, how glad they were to have them all back again. Polly began to sing, "Home,

Sweet Home," but before she finished the only
verse she knew, she wanted dinner, and Mary
opened the cage for her to come out. "Come
in," said Polly, which amused Mary very much,
as she could not very well get into Polly's
cage. Polly did not wait for Mary to try,
but jumped on her shoulder, to be taken
up-stairs. She walked about the room, while
Mary prepared for dinner; but rather interfered with Mary's toilet, as Mary had to stop
to laugh at her comical speeches and odd
way of putting her claw to her head, when
she seemed to think. Henry called to Mary
from his room, on a subject in which he was
always interested, that was, Mary's dress.
He always wanted her to wear bright colors
and gilt buttons, so, to-day, he called, "Mary,
are you going to wear your crimson dress to
dinner?"

"Oh, Henry," replied Mary, shutting her
eyes; "I don't know, I am trying not to think.
I want to dress as the flowers do."

"How is that?" asked Henry, who had not

heard the conversation which Mary had had with grandma.

"Why, Henry, they just wear what is best without thinking about it."

"Then," replied Henry, "dress like a crimson fuschia. You can dress her, Minny, and Mary can keep her eyes shut."

Mary, laughingly replied: "And what flower will you be like, Henry?"

"I will be a fruit," said Henry; "I will wear my plum-colored suit."

They were soon dressed, and, on opening the door where grandmamma was reading, Mary exclaimed: "Grandma, we are a fruit and a flower, guess what they are."

So grandma looked, and said: "If I look at your faces I should say a rosy-cheeked apple, and a rose-bud."

"No, grandma, not right, not right, try again."

"Then Henry must be a plum, is that right? and Mary a crimson rose-bud."

"You are right about Henry, but grandma,

I am a flower that bends down so," said Mary,
bending her head very far down.

" That's a fuschia," said grandma.. " I am
very glad to have my table so ornamented.
Grapes and oranges for the centre, and a
plum and a fuschia for the sides."

They thought it very wise in grandma to
guess, and had a great deal of talk about the
beauty and uses of fruits and flowers, which it
would take too long to tell you.

Dinner was not over till " dark time," as
Mary called it, as, on Sunday, grandma dined
at the usual time, five o'clock. This enabled
her to attend both services, and gave time for
all the servants to go in the morning, and
some of them in the afternoon. Grandma
then said she was ready to talk or to listen,
and as Mary generally had the most to say,
she asked for what grandma promised " about
those Israel children."

" Israel's children, or the Israelites," said
grandma, "were the children, and grand-
children, and so on, of Jacob, whose name

was also Israel. They were, for a long time, slaves in Egypt, but at last one of them (whose name was Moses), by the direction of God, led them away from Egypt towards a country called the Promised Land."

"Was that little Moses in the basket?" asked Mary.

"Yes," said grandma, "he was an Israelite, and chosen by God to take the people of Israel out of Egypt. You know about their crossing the Red Sea, and about Pharaoh's host being drowned; but do you remember what was the sign of God's presence with them?"

"Was it the 'cloudy pillar,' grandma?" said Henry.

"Yes, dear, that pillar of fire by night, and of cloud by day, led them over the sea, and through the country near it, to Mount Sinai. At Mount Sinai they stopped for a long time; and there they had manna given to them to eat, and there God gave them commandments, the same that we have now."

"Why, grandma, I think they have kept a long time," said Mary.

"A very long time," replied grandma. "And this very day, you and I try to obey them, just as the Israelites did."

"Oh, grandma, don't you wish you had heard God give them!" exclaimed Mary.

"Yes, dear ; but we might have been frightened by the thunder and lightning, and earthquake. The Israelites were, you remember, Henry."

"I'm rather glad I wasn't there," said Henry, for he did not like thunder storms ; "but please go on, grandma."

"After this they built a tabernacle or place of worship, and built it in a way that made it convenient to take it down, and carry it on their journeys."

"Were there no churches to go to, anywhere about the country ?" asked Mary.

"Not any. It was a wild, uncultivated country, with very few regular towns, and they were not like ours, with houses and churches," replied grandma.

"Oh, how very troublesome it would be, if we had to carry our churches about when we go travelling. Wouldn't it, Henry?"

"Rather," said he, laughing at the idea. "But, Mary, their church was made so it could take down easily. It was pillars standing up, and curtains over them instead of a wooden roof."

"No steeple and bell?" asked Mary.

"No, indeed, nothing of that kind. I'll ask papa to show you a picture of it, when we go home. Now, do let grandma go on."

"Inside of the tabernacle, was a beautiful wooden box, called an ark. On the lid, were two golden angels, and over it rested the pillar of cloud, looking like a mass of bright glory. When the time came for the Israelites to leave Mount Sinai, this bright glory floated off in front of the camp, and went before them all the time."

"Oh, grandma, how lovely! Don't you wish we had one?" exclaimed Mary.

"Would you always be ready to go wherever it led you, my darling children?" said grandma.

"I'm sure we should, grandma; and then we never should make any mistakes. I heard mamma say one day, 'I hope I am not mistaken;' now, if she could have seen the cloud, she would have known. Where did it take them to, grandma?"

"It took them to the Promised Land, and they were all ready to go into it. When they heard there were giants in the land, who would fight with them; then, instead of trusting to God to take care of them, they said they would go back to Egypt; and tried to stone some of the good men who wanted them to do right. They were a stiff-necked people, doing wrong."

"Oh, grandma, how dreadful. What happened then; did the giants get them?" asked Mary, with great interest.

" No, they were not where the giants were then ; but suddenly the bright cloud shone with a great glory, so that the people all saw it, and stood quite still. I suppose some of them had the stones in their hands all ready to throw. Then the Lord spoke to Moses."

" Oh, grandma, what *did* He say ?"

" He said the people of Israel must be punished. So He made them turn their backs upon the beautiful Promised Land, and go back to the wilderness for thirty-eight years."

" How dreadfully old they would be after that," exclaimed Mary.

" Some of them were very old then, and nearly all died in the wilderness, before they got back to the Promised Land. Only those who obeyed the Lord, and the children of the others, were saved. These children were men and women then, and they travelled up on the east side of the river Jordan, and set up their tabernacle on a beautiful plain, and en-camped there, under acacia trees, for a long time."

"Did the cloud stay there, and did they have those beautiful snow-storms of manna?" asked Mary, who always wanted all the particulars.

"Yes, dear, I am not sure that it was like a snow-storm, but probably looked a little so."

"And did they get their stiff necks cured?"

Here Henry gave one of his merry shouts of laughter; in which grandma had to join, rather unexpectedly to the earnest Mary.

"Oh, Mary, Mary, they hadn't really stiff necks; it means they were proud and bad," explained Henry, as soon as he could speak.

"It's figurative," said grandma, laughing.

"Figgertive again—I mean fig–u–ra–tive," said Mary.

"I think you will have to try to understand figurative language, dear Mary, but many little children make just such mistakes; it takes a great while to learn all that one wants to know. I knew a dear little girl, a very wise little girl, too. Her name was Lily, and I loved her very much. She asked once whether the Israelites had the rheumatism, for she heard the clergyman read about their stiff necks," replied grandma.

"Did she ; where has she gone ? I wish I knew her,"answered Mary.

"She has gone home, a great way off. We were very sorry to part with her, for she was kind and good, and knew a great deal about the Bible. I wish she were here now to play with you, but I must tell you a little more about the Israelites. While the Israelites were encamped, Moses repeated to them the laws that God had given. This took him a great many days. Then he appointed a leader for them named Joshua, and told them everything he could think of to help them to do right, to love God and to fear Him. After all this, he taught them a beautiful hymn, and they all sang it together, and then he lifted up his hands and blessed them ! and then, dear children, he went up into a mountain and died."

"Oh dear, grandma, why did he die, was he

sick, did he have to leave all the people ?" exclaimed Mary, with tears in her eyes.

"He had once in his life disobeyed the Lord, and though the Lord did not cease to love him, He said Moses must die before the Israelites went into the Promised Land. The time had come, and the Lord went with Moses up into the mountain, showed him the Beautiful Land, then Moses bade farewell to earth, and went to live forever in the immediate presence of Israel's God."

The children were quiet for a while, impressed perhaps with that wondrous death. Then Henry spoke with deep earnestness :

"Grandma, I would rather have such a guide as that pillar of cloud, than anything I can think of. I try so hard to do right about everything, but I so often forget, and do just what I am sorry for. Such a guide seems just what I need."

Grandma paused a moment, and then repeated to them these beautiful words :

"Just what they needed ! Wonderfully fitted
To meet the varying wants of every hour !
But oh ! how little did they prize the token
Of His unerring wisdom, love, and power !

" God's leadings often crossed their inclinations :
The pillar went too fast, or went too slow ;
It stayed too long, to suit their restless temper,
Or, when they wished to stay, it bade them go !

" It kept them so uncertain of the future !
It wrote 'IF GOD PERMIT' on every plan :
It seemed to mock the wisdom of the wisest,
And made a child of every full-grown man.

" To bear such discipline aright, they needed
Far more humility than they possessed ;
More self-abandonment, and more devotion,
A will surrendered, and a heart at rest.

" And so they murmured—murmured very often :
Their sullen hearts rebelled against the light :
And had not God been strong and very patient,
They never would have found their way aright.

" Now these things happened to them for ensamples
We find them 'written for our learning,' here :
O Israel ! Israel ! how can I condemn thee ?
Thy condemnation were my own, I fear !

" Yet, God of Israel, do not Thou forsake me !
Oh ! do not answer any wilful prayer,
But lead me safely to the land of promise,
To heaven itself, and I will praise Thee there !"

"Henry, dear, we have our Saviour, who said, 'Lo, I am with you alway, even unto the end of the world.' Pray earnestly for His guidance, trust Him to direct you, He will lead you, my dear children. Now, good-night. I must leave the history of the crossing of the Jordan for some other time."

Brightside.

XI.

About Going Home.

AT ten o'clock. precisely the sleigh came jingling to the door, and dear papa was in it. There were so many "Happy New-Years" wished, such a kissing and such a jumping with delight, that Polly, whose cage door was open, determined to be in the midst of it. She talked to herself, then suddenly flew to Mr. Montgomerie's shoulder, saying, "You dear old fellow, come in, come in, Happy New-Year, Home, sweet home, Polly put the kettle on."

"Why, Polly, old bird, how are you!" exclaimed her old friend, who had played many a merry game with her when he was a boy, as well as in later years.

"Pretty Poll, S'cat Jip, go to bed, Home sweet home," she went on. "S'cat Jip."

"Now, Polly, that wont do, I love my old Jip. Come here doggy, good dog, no matter about kissing me. Oh dear, what is a man to do with so many loving live creatures!" laughed papa, with a comical look of distress.

"Oh, poor papa, I'll help you. Here, Polly, come to me. Harry do take Jip and love him, so he wont think papa don't want him. He has had a long journey, Jippy, he loves you ever so much," said little Mary, trying to help everybody.

Papa then managed to take his overcoat off. "I'll hang it beside my old one, mother dear. You still keep that old remnant on the hat-stand, I see."

"Oh, papa, is that big shaggy thing yours? I hid in it on Saturday, and they were ever so long finding me," said Henry. "But, papa, how are we all to get in that little sleigh, and why did not Tom drive?"

"The large sleigh is broken, my boy, and

Tom has taken it for repairs. We are going to borrow grandma's 'family mansion' to go home in," answered papa, with one of his merry looks.

"Really, papa, do you mean that funny old thing that we play in? I heard Susan call it the 'family mansion,' one day. Why, it's broken."

"My dear son, how absurd you are. The new sleigh is at your service, the old mansion has not been used for years," said grandma, laughing at the idea.

"Well, mother, I'll do as you say, but I really would like once more to have a sleighing frolic in that old 'get along,' as I used to call it. Do have it put in order for me." She promised its restoration, and then they all went into the library, and gathered around the fire. Presently Henry left the room, calling Mary and Polly to come out.

"What do you want, brother?" asked his sister.

"I thought, maybe, grandma and papa

might want to have a little talk without us, you know ; so as we are not to go till after lunch, we shall have time to go down to the farm-yard, and you can see that proud old rooster, and the muscovy ducks."

Polly had to stay at home, but Jip went rollicking with them, over the snowy paths. While they were gone, Mr. Montgomerie said : "I hope that our little birds have not tired you with their constant chattering, dear mother."

"No, my son, they have been only a comfort. When they have permission to talk, they go on like a rushing stream, but the very moment I have anything to do, or propose books, or quiet plays they yield at once. I never saw happier or more thoroughly obedient children. Your mode of education has been successful, so much '*do*,' and so little '*don't.*' I think that the way in which some children are teased by 'don't do this' and 'don't do that,' must be hard for them to bear."

"I suppose we should have to say 'don't,' if

our children were always trying to do wrong, but we certainly do try to keep their lives full of right. There was a great lesson taught in the parable of the house swept and garnished and *empty*, in which seven evil spirits went to dwell, and also in the old words, 'Satan finds some mischief still for *idle* hands to do.' Our children are always earnestly occupied, even their plays are earnestly enjoyed. Then they are so strong and well. I cannot blame others for different treatment of their children. An ailing child would require a very different kind of management," he replied.

"My dear Henry, I can only repeat, Thank God for your wife and children !"

"I do, mother dear, and thank Him for a faithful, untiring mother."

Lunch was served, and made a very important meal as preparatory to the journey home. Then Mary made a flying excursion round the house to say good-bye to the servants, particularly to old Susan, grandma's maid, with whom Mary was a great favorite. Then the

wrappings were put on, and from the midst
of shawls and furs, dear grandma was kissed,
and thanked for the lovely visit. Jip was
hugged till he could hardly breathe. Polly
was told to be good, and take care of grandma, and finally the merry little. ones were
packed into the sleigh.

There were so many questions to ask
about mamma, and then about the little dogs,
and the pony, that papa had as much as he
could do to answer. He let them talk, till
the rush was over, and then asked :

" Now, what have you learned in these
three days ? Never forget that *something*
must be learned *every* day."

" I know," said Mary ; "each day—

> ' We must learn something useful,
> We must do something kind,
> We must see something beautiful.'

That's the rule, isn't it papa ?"

" Yes, dear, but all that I want to know is
about the useful and the beautiful ; the kind

things that you do, you can keep in your own little hearts."

"I learned subterranean, comfortable and figurative, how the flowers live, and lots about the Israel children, about manna, and Jesus the Rock, and—and the cloud. Now Henry you tell," said Mary.

"I think I learned all that Mary did, dear papa, and I hope I learned something I do not know how to explain, about looking up to that Guiding Cloud, and how the Israelites had to watch it so as to be ready to journey. It made me think of, 'Be ye also ready,' and I want to watch as they did."

"I understand you, my boy, that is one of the heart lessons. And what did you find that was beautiful?"

"So much, papa, I don't know where to begin : the very, very blue sky, for one thing, and the snow drifts. I noticed them on Sunday. The wind had blown under the snow, and it hung over and made a blue shadow," replied Henry.

"And oh, Henry, the rooster's tail, and the ducks' heads," exclaimed Mary.

"Yes, papa, they shone so in the sun. I think what the sun makes us see, is so wonderful. The roosters' long green feathers glistened so in the light, and the ducks' heads were like green gold," said Henry.

"And, papa, the frost on the window panes just like leaves," said Mary.

"Then, papa, I don't know whether it is 'beautiful,' but there is something about the way that grandma does everything, as if she felt every movement and word in her heart, I do not explain it very well, but as I look at her, I *think* 'how beautiful!'" said Henry.

"I know what you mean, my boy, though that was not what I intended when I told you to look for beautiful things; but it is also beautiful, and is what we call moral beauty. It is grandma's earnestness that you admire."

"If those things are beautiful, I think the way Jip loves grandma is beautiful. I don't think he is beautiful outside, but he can't bear to have grandma out of his sight," said Mary, nodding her head in a very wise way.

Papa laughed, and began to talk about some merry subject, for he did not approve of too much thinking for such young heads.

They were soon home, and dear mamma was rejoiced to see her bright little sunbeams again.

"Take off your wraps down here," she said. "Then go up-stairs into the nursery and into Henry's dressing-room, and see how you like the new doors."

A rush was made up-stairs at these words, first into the nursery, which they did not stop to look at, but ran through it to Henry's door. Screams of delight were heard by papa and mamma, who waited in the up-stairs hall.

"Oh, what a lovely room ! See, Mary, I am to sleep here, in this dear little bed ; and see the pictures, and this little book-case !"

"And oh, Harry, the beautiful carpet, fuschias all over it, and this funny look-ing-glass down to the floor with piles of ·.

drawers each side, and a dear little mat between ; and see the wash-stand, fuschias all over the pitcher and basin. Oh, I never, never, never, did see anything so beautiful ! Do you think I may open this door into mamma's dressing-room ?"

" Oh, yes," said Henry, " I am sure we may, because mamma said ' doors,' you know."

" Oh, Henry, Henry, another room ! Just like your's, only all different. It must be for me." Here she ran back to the nursery. " It is Harry, it is, it is, for both beds are gone. Now we've each got a room !"

" So it is, you dear little sister. You've got the same little bed, and the same looking-glass with such ducks of drawers, and another little mat, only yours is blue, and mine is crimson."

" And see Harry, my carpet has blue flowers, and oh, dear, my pitcher and basin have forget-me-nots on them, and there's my little doll's bedstead right by mine, and see my pictures, they are all different from yours.

Oh, look, I've got the 'Glory Song ;' see the angels and the shepherds, and that light coming down, and the shepherds looking up, and the precious little sheep, oh, Harry !"

"My picture is all light too. I wonder what it is. See, Mary, a door open, and light inside, and angels, and look, all flowers. Why, it's a garden ! See the women looking surprised. Oh, I know, it's the tomb of our Saviour. Don't you remember it was in a garden ?" said Henry, earnestly examining the picture which hung opposite to his bed.

"No, Henry, I don't know at all ; don't let's worry over the pictures yet. See, all my clothes are in my drawers, and I've got a little closet. Have you, Henry ? with low down hooks. The rooms are perfect ; come, let's tell mamma and papa."

At this, Mr. and Mrs. Montgomerie, and Minny, with her bright eyes and happy face, came forward from the nursery.

"Thank you, thank you, dear papa and mamma !" exclaimed both children.

"These little rooms are your New-Year's presents," said mamma, "from papa and me. Everything in them is useful and plain, and bright too, with pictures and flowers. You are to keep everything in order in them, and you are to play in the nursery, where you will find all your playthings ready for you."

"Yes, mamma, we will; it will be easy enough to keep them nice. Please tell me," said Henry, "about this picture. I do not quite understand it."

"It is a picture of the tomb of Jesus, on that beautiful morning, when He had risen. Read the words under the picture : 'Come, see the place where the Lord lay.' The Saviour is not there, the women are looking for Him, and the angels seem to be telling them, 'He is not here, for He is risen.' There are beautiful flowers all about, for His tomb was in a garden, and everything is bright, from the glory which shone from the countenance of the angel. Mary's picture is about the coming of Christ, and yours, about His rising from the tomb. We will talk more about them, another day. Now, show Minny all the new things, and then come down to papa and me, in the dining-room."

Minny and the children looked over all the new possessions, with increasing pleasure ; discussed the pictures, not only those about the Bible subjects, but the one about the little ducks, sailing on the pond, and the one where the kittens are playing with the pendulum of the clock ; and that one, which was in Henry's room, about the cat and the dog. Perhaps you have never seen it, so I will tell you about it.

The picture represents a nice clean kitchen. On a bench are seated a wise looking cat, and a merry looking dog, both sitting up on their hind legs, and looking at a little girl standing before them. She is cutting a slice of bread from a loaf, for their breakfast, and saying : " Don't be impatient, children."

This picture they laughed over a good deal ; finally, Henry said : " Minny, don't you

10

think these little rooms have a very happy look ?"

" Blessings on you, dear chil'n, sure I do. Dey's de happiest looking little rooms I ever did see. 'Spect you'll keep 'em dredful nice ; dey's dredful happy looking, sure nuff," replied Minny, nodding her turban.

A call from mamma made the children run down-stairs to the dining-room, where they found dinner prepared for them, although it was not four o'clock.

" We are going to have a dinner-party, to-day," said mamma, " and I have had your dinner early, so that I can be with you ; for you will have to entertain yourselves this evening, dear birdies."

"Are we not to come down at dessert ?" asked Mary.

" No, dear," replied mamma.

Mary waited a few moments, occupying herself with her soup, but hoping mamma would tell her why not. As mamma said nothing, Mary thought she would venture to say :

"Mamma, Mr. Williams *always* lets Julia and Fanny go down to dessert."

Mamma said : "What of that, dear Mary?"

Mary was a little confused, but said in reply, "I did not see why *we* could not."

"I have a good reason, my little girl. Can you not trust your mother?" was the reply.

"Yes, mamma, but"—

Mary did not finish her sentence, for just then she saw William bring in some of her favorite dishes, and on the side-table prepared for the dessert, the white grapes, and oranges, of which she was especially fond, and she could not say any more about it.

Mrs. Montgomerie helped her as carefully and lovingly as ever ; and papa, who had been reading, began to tell them a comical story ; so no more was said on the subject.

When dinner was over, they went outside with their sleds for an hour's play before dark, and had a very merry time, quite forgetting the dinner-party. When they came in, they looked at the dining-table, set for twelve guests, ran to see if mamma looked beautiful—which they thought she did, and then to Minny in the nursery, where there was a bright light and plenty of playthings to amuse them, until eight o'clock.

While the guests were arriving, the children had a nice talk with Minny. She always had something pleasant to tell them : and the nursery was a cheerful place, and a room very full of happy times.

Soon Mary said, " There they go into the dining-room. What a nice time grown-up people do have."

" I tink chil'n hab de best time," said Minny. " Dere ain't no 'sponsibility, dey just enjoys deirselves. Just now you see all de care de Missis has. Tink ob dem rooms ; she has been weeks and weeks a fixin ob dem, and you jest walks in, and has dem all ready to your hand."

" Yes," said Henry, "and how papa has to go to the city, two or three times every week.

He is so tired when he comes home, that I wish I could go for him."

" What does he go for ?" asked Mary.

" Why, I suppose to get money to pay for things," said Henry.

" He ought to bring up a box full, so that it would last longer, then he need not go so often. I'll tell him so, some day," said Mary.

" Maybe he has to *make* the money," said Henry. " I don't know exactly about it."

" He *couldn't* make it, I know that very well. Why, Harry, money is printed paper, with pictures on ; I've seen lots of it. There's somebody smoking a pipe on one paper of money. Oh, there's all kinds, and there are silver pieces : he can't make such things, people must give it to him," replied Mary.

Minny laughed heartily at this wise talk about money, and said : " I 'spect dere's different ways of making money. Some folks sells things. I think you'd better ask your father about it, and now hab a nice play of something anudder."

They did have a nice play, and had quite forgotten the party, when they heard the parlor door open and mamma's voice with that of a friend approaching their room.

"There is that nice Miss Sables coming up-stairs. Oh, I hope she will come in here!" exclaimed Mary.

The door opened, and "that nice Miss Sables," with her bright face,. and cheery voice, and quick step, did come in.

"Good evening, dear children! good evening, Minny. Sit down, Minny, I've come to pay you all a little visit. Your mother said you were not coming down this evening, and, therefore, I had to come up and see you. Mohammed and the mountain, you know. Now, Mrs. Montgomerie, you need not wait for me, I'm going to make a long visit, I want the children all to myself."

Mamma laughed, and returned to her other guests, leaving Miss Sables in a comfortable arm-chair by the fire with the children, one on each side of her. Miss Sables was a great friend of theirs, and one of their greatest pleasures was to visit her in her beautiful cottage in the village. So they were much delighted that she had taken the trouble to come up to their nursery.

"Oh, Miss Sables, as soon as you are rested, will you please come and look at our new rooms, our New Year's presents from papa and mamma," said Mary.

"Rested, my dear child! pray what has tired me? Show them to me right away, I love to see new things!" she answered, springing up in the liveliest manner.

Minny lighted the candles on each side of the little bureaus, "piles of drawers," Mary had called them, and everything was explained to Miss Sables. She was much delighted, and said she wished she was a little girl again. No, she thought she would rather be a little boy. In fact, she did not know which she liked best, but she was sure she would like just such a little room.

"Yes, indeed," said Henry; "but to be

quite happy you would want my papa and mamma, too. You know it makes more happiness when they put all these things here for us."

"Indeed you are right, my child, and did they choose all these lovely pictures?"

"Yes, they did ; Mary's Bible picture is the Glory Song, and mine is the Rising of Christ," answered Henry.

"That reminds me," said their friend, "I saw you at Sunday-school, on Christmas morning. Now, on Easter Sunday, I want you to come again, and to sit with my class, and to answer, too. We are going to have a lesson on the Resurrection of Christ."

"But how can we learn it?" asked Mary.

"My dear, I will tell you. You know Matthew, Mark, Luke and John, I suppose," said Miss Sables, in her quick way.

The children were a little puzzled about knowing them, but Henry answered : "Do you mean the Bible books, ma'am?"

"Certainly I do. Matthew, Mark, Luke,

and John wrote the four gospels. They were friends and followers of our Lord, and the gospels are the books they wrote about Him. Do you understand ?"

" Oh, yes," said Mary, " we know *that*, but I thought you meant to ask whether we had spoken to them."

" Not at all, not at all, my dear ! I did not suppose you were ' wandering Jews.' No, not at all. Now, this being plain, you must read in the latter part of each of these books about the burial and rising of Christ. Learn all you can about the subject, and when you come, answer what you know. You will enjoy it, I think. We shall have lovely flowers, and everything joyful."

" That will be splendid," said Henry ; " we will do the best we can. Perhaps papa will teach us on Sundays, so that we shall be ready."

" I've no doubt he will. Now let us sit down again, I want to tell you about the Indians," said Miss Sables, returning to the nursery.

"Oh, dear!" said Mary, "those people with feathers in their heads? I hope they are not coming here."

"Coming here! I'm sure I said nothing of the kind. I hope not, indeed, but we have sent missionaries out to them, and these missionaries have written to us that the poor Indians need clothes very much, and I am going to collect all I can, then I will put them in a barrel, and send it to them; now I want you both to help me."

"Indeed we will," said Henry, "if you will tell us how."

"There are many things that you can do. Mary can sew, and can make little aprons and calico dresses for the Indian babies; you can both give some of your money. You, Henry, can cut long strips of old linen and flannel for bandages, and roll them very tight. You can show him, Minny."

"'S'pect I'll do it sure, ma'am," said Minny; "we have dredful sight ob old linen. De chil'n and me will send a lot of tings, please ma'am.

"Thank you, thank you, Minny. I knew you would help I want to send my barrel in about two weeks; whenever you are ready send the articles to me: now I have had a delightful visit. You must come soon and see me. Ask mamma to let you come to tea; we will have a nice little supper of oysters and waffles, say next Thursday. I will send for that spotted child that you are so fond of, Sorella, if your mamma has no objection, and we will play blindman's buff, and have a good frolic. What do you say?"

"Thank you, thank you, dear Miss Sables. I am sure mamma will let us come. Would you *please* ask Jocko, too?" earnestly said Mary.

"Certainly, my dear; pray have you a pet rhinoceros you would like to bring? Only be happy, tea at six, don't eat any dinner that day, or you will have no appetites. Now I must go. Good-bye."

"Good-bye, good-bye," said the children.

Minny closed the door. It opened suddenly. Miss Sables looked in once more: "Did I say tea at six? no, half-past six, don't forget the rhinoceros," and she was gone.

"Isn't she just too nice for anything!" exclaimed Henry. "Oh, I hope mamma will let us go. Why can't everybody be merry like her, instead of stupid, like Mrs. ——?"

"Don't s'pect it's good to talk 'bout what odder folks isn't, Mas'r Harry," said Minny. "Miss Sables is dre'dful nice, dat's certain."

"What did she mean about the Nossyrus?" asked Mary.

"Oh, that was only her fun. It's some kind of a big animal," answered Henry.

"Now, child'ns, it's nearly eight o'clock. Let's sing something, and then you can try de new little beds," said Minny.

"Sing, 'Little drops of water,'" said Mary.

They sang their little hymn together, and then each one repeated a verse from the Bible. "Say whatever you like de best," said Minny.

"I think I like best of all the verses, 'The Lord is in His holy Temple, let all the earth keep silence before Him.'" Henry repeated it, slowly and solemnly.

"That is beautiful !" said Mary ; "but I like best of all, 'The evening and the morning were the first day.' There is something about it so comfortable and sure."

"It's a good verse for to-day, the first day of the year," said Henry, thoughtfully. "I think your verse said first, and mine next, seem to sound fine. What's your's, Minny. Then we'll try them all together."

"'Looking for that blessed hope, and de glorious appearing of de great God and our Saviour Jesus Christ,'" said Minny, trying to pronounce very plainly.

"Now," said Henry, "listen to them straight on."

"'And the evening and the morning were the first day.'"

"'The Lord is in His holy Temple, let all the earth keep silence before Him.'"

"'Looking for that blessed hope and the

glorious appearing of the great God and our Saviour, Jesus Christ.'"

"Don't they go nicely together? I think they are lovely. Minny, mamma said we were to pray by ourselves at night, beside our own little beds, and after we are in bed, you are to come in and put out our candles. Now, Mary, you go into your room. You may go through my room to-night, but generally you must go in by the hall door."

"Yes, brother dear, and oh, how I wish we could see darling mother one more minute."

The darling mother came up just at this crisis, and kissing them good-night, hoped they would sleep well in the new rooms. She had only time for this, as her guests had not gone. The children were soon asleep, gaining strength for another happy day.

XII.

About the Tea-Party and other things.

"GO to bed, and get up, go to bed, and get up, and then the tea-party!" exclaimed Mary, partly to herself, as she was preparing for dinner, on Tuesday, the day after New-Year's. "Wont it be lovely, Harry, to go to tea at Miss Sables'?"

"Yes, indeed!" called Henry from his room, "wasn't it good in mamma to say we might go?"

"Ye-es," returned Mary, doubtfully, "but Harry, if we had been grown-up people, we should just have said, 'Certainly, Miss Sables, we will come with pleasure,' and not asked anybody."

"But we are not 'grown-up people,' and we don't always know what is best for us. I would rather papa and mamma should tell me what to do," said Henry, decidedly.

Mary opened the door between the rooms, and said, in a low voice : "I wanted 'ticularly to go to dessert yesterday, and I think mamma might have told me *why* we could not."

"Oh, Mary! sister dear," exclaimed Henry, "don't say such words Dear mamma knows best. She is our guiding cloud, far up high above us. We can trust *her* to lead us. I can't exactly say what I mean, but it seems to me as if she could see better than we can."

Mary stood perfectly still for a moment, looking earnestly at her brother ; then, to his great surprise, ran out into the hall, where she had heard her father's step. She seized his hand, drew him into his room, exclaiming : "Oh, papa, papa, I have seen something *so* beautiful, it's my beautiful sight for to-day. I wish you could see it, but it's over now," and Mary closed her eyes as if she would recal her " beautiful sight."

"My dear child," said her father, " what

is the matter with you—what have you seen?

"Oh dear, dear!" said Mary, "it was Harry—you know, papa, I've been a little *think* naughty, not punish naughty, but the kind that comes first, naughty in my heart. It was about dessert, because mamma would not let us go down to the party yesterday, and I was a little scrap angry, even to-day. I said something about it to Harry, and oh, papa, he said we could trust mamma, she was up high where she could see, like a guiding cloud, and there came such a light in his eyes, and such a beauty look on his face, that if I had not heard you I would have cried out loud," and here she threw her arms around papa's neck, and did cry, but not loud, only soft, gentle tears.

Papa held her in his arms for a few minutes, and then said: "Thank you, my darling, for telling me. Harry is right, you may safely trust your mother, she can see dangers for her children, when you little ones think all is

11

safe. *Trust her*, not only now, but as long as she is here to guide you."

As Mr. Montgomerie prepared for dinner, and little Mary sat quietly in his arm-chair waiting for him, he thought about what Mary had told him, and remembered the words, " Saw his face, as it had been the face of an angel." Then he thought how the feelings that are in the heart are shown in the face, and he wondered if every one would be lovely to look at, if their hearts were always full of love and kindness. Whilst his mind was interested in such ideas, Henry came to the door, as he said, " to find out what had become of everybody," but Henry did not know why papa put his arms around him, and called him his " dear, dear boy."

They went to dinner after this, and all went on as usual until Thursday, which came at last ; and by six o'clock, Henry, Mary, Sorella and Jocko, attended by Minny, reached the cottage door.

" I'm so glad you came at six ; come right

in by the fire, tea is all ready. I forgot to ask
if Jocko can eat oysters! how are you all?
Minny, put everything out in the hall, and
don't come back for the children till nine
o'clock. Nine is a proper hour for everything
to break up. Oh, what cold little faces!
'tschick, it makes me sneeze to kiss you."
So Miss Sables talked on, in her merry way,
while the children struggled out of their wrappings, and warmed their cold faces, and Jocko
seated himself on the mantel-shelf, where he
could see everybody.

" Now for tea. If you warm yourselves any
more you will melt away. Come into the
dining-room. Give me your arm, Master
Harry, and Mary bring Sorella. There! Harry
opposite to me, and one young lady on each
side. Jocko, stand beside your mistress. Now
we are all happy."

" Miss Sables," said Mary, "I didn't bring
any Nossyrus."

" I'm delighted to hear it, my dear, for he
would have had his tea in the large, cold

parlor, unless, indeed, he had chosen to eat
us, which would have been very probable. It
was very hazardous in me to invite him.
Take more oysters, Sorella. So Jocko likes
cake, does he? Here, you little quadruped,
take this sugar. Harry, if you don't ask me
to have some chicken salad, I will never
forgive you," said Miss Sables, laughing.

"Oh do, do," said Henry, "you may have
it all," helping her very nicely.

"Thank you, thank you, one spoonful is
enough. Sorella, how is your grandfather?"

"He is not quite as well as usual, thank
you, ma'am, but he sleeps so much that Mrs.
Jones said he would not miss me this evening,
and I was so glad to come."

"I am very glad you did, my dear, it will
be a little change for you. It is not very lively
in our village in the winter. Now, Mary,
what about the Indian babies?"

"Minny and I have made two little canton
flannel night-wrappers, and deranged a good
deal of other work," answered Mary.

"Doubtless," said Miss Sables, laughing. "I am very glad to hear about the wrappers; and you, Master Harry, what have you done?"

"I've cut, or torn, a hundred yards of strips for bandages, and rolled them tight, the way Minny showed me. She said her mistress used to keep them all ready to use when the servants were hurt. What do the Indians want them for, ma'am?" replied Henry.

"Oh, my dear, when they break their legs and arms, and their children's heads, and for any other little accidents. I never should have thought of sending bandages, but they were asked for, in one of the letters from a missionary, and I want my barrel to contain a little of everything," answered their friend.

"Will you please tell me who the Indians are?" said Sorella. "Grandfather was always expecting to meet them, and yet I never saw one."

"Just like a foreigner," said Miss Sables, laughing. "I believe we are supposed to be

set in a framework of arrows and tomahawks.
You may never see an Indian, my dear, to
know him. There is one living near here
who makes baskets, but as he neither wears
feathers nor paint, he looks like any one else.
You asked about the Indians. They were the
original inhabitants of our country, but have
gradually disappeared from among the white
people, and though a few remain among us,
the greater number are living in the western
part of our country. Some of them are quite
wild and uncivilized. It is to these Indians of
our western states that our missionaries have
gone. The missionaries are good Christians,
who devote their lives to preaching, and
teaching ignorant people about the love of
our Saviour.

The barrel, of which we were speaking, is to
be filled with clothing for them; for our
Saviour taught us to do kindnesses for the poor,
as well as to teach them. St. James says it
does not profit to say, ' Be ye warmed and
fed,' unless you really give ' those things

which are needful to the body.' Do you understand me, my dear children ?"

"Oh yes, ma'am," said Sorella, "maybe Carlotta will see some Indians."

"Who is 'Carlotta,' and where has she gone ?" asked Miss Sables.

"Carlotta is grandfather's grand-daughter," replied Sorella ; "her husband took her to the West."

"But, my dear, if she is your grandfather's grand-daughter, is she not your sister ?" asked Miss Sables.

"No, ma'am," replied Sorella, "grandfather says he is not my real relation, he adopted me.".

"Ahem !" said Miss Sables, looking wise. "Is every one done ? Come, now for Blind-man's-buff, or Proverbs, or What is my thought like. Which will you play ?"

Blind-man's-buff was decided upon. The tables and chairs were moved aside, Jocko went up on the cornice, and made faces at them, and then Miss Sables and the children played, until they were tired with running and laughing.

"Oh, dear," laughed Mary, as she caught Miss Sables, "you're a great deal nicer than a little girl."

"Thank you, thank you. I'm easier to catch, I know, because I am larger; but do let us rest awhile," returned her friend.

Proverbs were tried next, but it was nine o'clock before the fun was half over, and papa arrived in the midst of a great clapping of hands, as Henry guessed a proverb.

"That's because I'm coming!" said Mr. Montgomerie, as he entered. "I deserve to be clapped, for coming out such a cold night."

"So you do, my friend. Come in by the fire. You're a brave man, and I am delighted to see you," said Miss Sables, placing a chair in front of her bright wood fire.

"Thank you, I will for a few minutes; but I must take the children at once. It is a bitter night for Tom and the horses. The stars look like diamonds, and winkle and twinkle, as if it were too cold to keep their eyes open," he replied, trying to help the children with their cloaks and hoods.

" My dear Mr. Montgomerie !" exclaimed Miss Sables, " pray content yourself with being ornamental ! You are putting Mary's cloak on upside down ; let me attend to the children."

" Do be sorry for me," said Mr. Montgomerie in a helpless sort of way, taking his seat again. " I'm unfortunately a man, you know, and don't know how to dress little girls."

Jocko jumped down from his high station to Mr. Montgomerie's shoulder, and began chattering to him. They all laughed at this unexpected consolation, which Mr. Montgomerie pretended to accept with much gratitude ; whispering to Miss Sables, " little brother, do you think ?"

" Don't introduce such ideas in my cottage, my good friend. God created man in His own image," answered Miss Sables, with intense gravity.

" Thank God, for His sure word of truth,"
replied Mr. Montgomerie. "No one will go
astray, my friend, with that guide. The books
of nature and of revelation have but one
author. May we live to see the whole earth
filled with His knowledge."

The children had no idea what their elders
were talking about, or why their merriment
had turned so suddenly to seriousness. Mary,
as usual, thought it was "getting to be a little
like school;" but she said nothing, as she helped
Sorella with her wrappings; and as soon as
they were ready, Miss Sables was as bright as
ever, kissing them good-bye, and thanking
them for being so agreeable.

"Say good-bye to Jocko," said Mary, who
had an indefinite idea that Jocko had been
slighted.

"Good-bye, quadruped," said Miss Sables.
"You have behaved very well for a monkey.
Now, children, come again soon. Don't forget
the Indians."

The frosty air made Miss Sables shut the

door on her last words, and the children enjoyed their starlight drive, and their own accounts of the evening so much, that they were sorry when it was over. All pleasant days have an end, as well as unpleasant ones ; and it was not long before Blind-man's-buff, and Miss Sables, were remembered in dreams.

One morning, soon after Miss Sables's tea-party, while the family were at breakfast, William entered with a note for Mrs. Montgomerie, to which an answer was required. She read it hastily, and said :

" Tell James to say to Mrs. Montgomerie that I will be there at two o'clock."

When William left the room, she proposed to read the note aloud. It was from grandma, and was as follows :

" DEAR LOUISE :

" For some time, I have been surprised to see that Sorella's hair has evidently been dyed. It is growing out a beautiful brown, instead of the reddish black which made her look so oddly, and, in the daytime, the difference is very evident. Her complexion is also changing from a dark hue, to a fair and fine skin. In some places, it is so

light that she looks spotted. That there is something
wrong about the child,. I am convinced ; and have wished to
speak to Mariano, her grandfather, about it. but the difficulty in his understanding English increases daily. After
he recovered his speech, from the paralysis, he seemed to
forget how to talk in English ; although he told me in
looks, that he understood what I said to him ; but now he
has forgotten even that, and we only converse by Sorella's
help. Yesterday she told me, that her grandfather wished
to tell something before he died, and asked if any one understood Italian. I told her to say that I could find some
one. To which he replied, that he would like to have
what he said, written down before a witness. I promised
to arrange all for him. And now, my dear daughter, if you
will do this for me, and meet me at two o'clock, I shall be
very much indebted to you. If Henry has not gone to the
city, ask him to come and write what is said ; if he has, I
will do that part myself. I am sure, there is a mystery
about that refined, lovely child, which may then be explained. Love to each dear one,

"ELLEN B. MONTGOMERIE."

"How very strange," said Mrs. Montgomerie ; " Sorella may have been stolen from
her parents. You know how impressed we
have all been with her refined and. gentle
manner. What a blessing it would be, if we
could be the means of restoring her."

"You have gone on, dear wify, with a hop,
skip, and a jump. Sorella seems to me like a

genuine Italian. She is a graceful little thing, but some of the Italian peasants are remarkable for refined bearing. However, I will do the writing for mother's new charge, if you will translate his Italian."

The children were much excited on the subject, and Sorella became an object of deep interest. Mrs. Montgomerie requested them not to speak about it, excepting to each other, until something more definite was known; adding: "I'm sure we can trust you, because you understand that it is best that Sorella should not know about it, until we are quite certain, and the only way to keep a secret, is not to tell *anyone*."

"Mariano is a very interesting old man," said Mr. Montgomerie; "and has been much benefited by mother's ministrations. What an earnest worker she is! I thought, when she undertook to reform the poor-house, that for once she would fail. But those clean and happy people, their joyful voices in their daily hymns, are a lesson against despair."

"Papa," said Henry, "doesn't grandma ever get tired?"

"Certainly, my son.   Do you know how she rests?"

"No, papa, I suppose she lies down, like other tired people."

"My dear boy, did you ever see her lie down 'like other people.'"

"No, papa, never.   But I have seen her look very tired, and lean back in the arm-chair, and say 'Now, dear children, be quiet, for three minutes, by the clock,—that will rest me.'   After that, she would be up again as bright as ever."

"That is not at all like other people is it, my boy?   Another way grandma rests, is to change her occupations.   I have often seen her rest from reading by sewing, and from sewing by writing.   She repeats,

> ' A *want* of occupation is not rest,   .
> A mind quite vacant, is a mind distrest.'

That three minutes in the arm-chair, was an extreme case."

"How wonderful the effect of her example

is," said Mrs. Montgomerie; "every one is incited to do something where she is. Do you remember old Mr. Scanning, who said, when he was visiting her: 'I must go away, Ellen, you will set me to work if I stay,' and mother's characteristic answer, 'Oh, don't go, I want you to give some legal advice to Mrs. Herndon about that mortgage on the mill.' His laugh astonished mother as he said, 'I thought so. I ought to have gone away last night,' then when she understood him, her merry laugh was good to hear. She enters into the joys and sorrows of every one, and yet preserves her own individuality thoroughly."

"Well," said Mary, "I suppose grandma is all those hard words, but the best thing about her is, that she loves to play as well as we do, doesn't she, Harry?"

"Yes, every bit as well, she's a great deal jollier than those little girls and boys at—"

"Stop, my boy, do not make comparisons. One person does one thing well, another person another," said papa.

"But, papa," said Mary, "grandma does *everything* well ; that's how she is so indifferent from every other 'vidual."

"Exactly," replied her father, with one of his comical looks ; "there could be nothing clearer ; only the ' in ' got in the wrong place. Now, little ones, I think a very patient governess has been waiting nine minutes for you, good-bye. I want to have a little talk with mamma."

The children obeyed at once, and as they ran off, Henry's foot tripped on a little mat which lay at the parlor door, they having chosen ' the longest way round.' He fell, and a crash was heard.

"Oh !" exclaimed Mrs. Montgomerie ; "I hope that is not the Bohemian vase."

"Mamma, mamma !" exclaimed Henry, in tones of deepest sorrow, "can you forgive me ? I have broken your beautiful Bohemian vase."

A deep crimson flush passed over the face of his mother, for this vase was something very rare and choice. It was but for a moment.

"*Forgive* you, my boy! for what? You surely did not intend to do it," said she.

"Oh, no, indeed, mamma, I fell over the mat, and put out my hand without meaning to do any harm, but it struck the little table, and threw it over—do, do forgive me."

"My dear boy, I have nothing to forgive. I am very sorry the beautiful vase is broken, and more sorry that you have had the pain of breaking it. Now, tell William to gather the pieces of glass carefully, and to re-arrange the room. Do not think about it again, except to remember that it is safer to *walk* through rooms where there are door-mats and vases!"

Henry and Mary walked very soberly up-stairs.

"Mary," said Henry, "did you ever think how very lovely and kind mamma is?"

"No," replied Mary; "I never thinked about it at all, I just love her."

"But, Mary, she is so different from mothers in books ; they are *so* angry when their children break things."

"They must be very bad mothers," said Mary.

"Oh, no, not bad, only impatient, you know, that kind of angry I mean. I read in a newspaper about a little boy who broke a vase, and his mother was *so* impatient, and soon after, he was drowned, and she was so unhappy, she fainted or died, I don't know which, only she came to life again, and there was her child not drowned at all, and she was so glad and happy she never was impatient to him any more."

"Oh, wasn't that good?" said Mary. "Do you think it was true ? Papa says newspaper stories are not true."

"This was, though, because it was in one of those papers that papa reads on Sunday, and it told the names and everything."

"I'm glad our mamma isn't one of the kind they have in books and papers ; that's what I have thinked about it."

"Mary, *I* think you ought to say 'thought,' instead of 'thinked.'"

"I will, if you want me to, Harry, but thinked sounds the rightest. How hard it is to talk! I am always saying some wrong word."

"You try to say such hard ones. I don't know what you mean sometimes," he answered.

"I don't either," said Mary; "I think I do when I begin, but after I have said them, they sound so strange I'm all 'wildered. The duchess would say the moral of it is, 'It is better finish before you begin.'"

"Come, come, chatter-boxes," said the voice of the governess. The door closed, and for several hours there was quiet at Brightside.

At two o'clock Mr. and Mrs. Montgomerie were in the room of the Italian organ-grinder. He was supported by pillows, and looked very feeble, and was obliged to stop and rest many times during the account which he gave. He was a gentle-minded old man, and his story

interested his hearers very much.   There was
an evidence of its truth in the quaint simplicity
with which it was told, and which Mrs. Montgomerie tried to preserve in the translation.
Mr. Montgomerie wrote it down as his wife
translated it, but it is too long for this chapter.

XIII.

The Organ-Grinder's Story.

"MY name is Mariano Zachiti. I was born in Amalfi, and I must be nearly eighty years old. When I was a young man I was a courier, but gave that occupation up to go and live with my mother, who was too old to take care of herself. When she died I married, and I was a very happy, and a good man, while my wife was alive.

"We lived in Cetara, near Amalfi, and supported ourselves by fishing. We had one little girl. She was very beautiful, and had a fine voice. She used to sing in Amalfi and Salerno. Her mother or I always went with her, and we made more money by her voice than we ever did by fishing. We were all happy then. Our daughter married when she was thirteen years old, and, soon after that, my wife, my Mariti, died. I was very wicked then. I was angry because she was taken from me, but I was nearly crazed with grief. I hope I shall be forgiven for that sin.

" Some years after that, my daughter came home to die. Her husband had left her, she supported herself and her child by sewing for the shops in Naples; but, at last, her health failed, and she came back to her old home, bringing her little girl of four years of age. It was a great comfort to have them with me, and I went to my fishing again to do the best I could for my dying daughter. The neighbors were kind, and staid with her while I was absent. The little girl seemed to know that she, too, must help, and for a few months the old house seemed like home again. The vines, which, in my sorrow, I had torn down, began to grow over the doorway, and the flowers to bloom; so I knew that Mariti was pleased with me, for I was trying to do right, and to support her child. At last the day

came that Mariti wanted Carlotta, (I am
speaking as I used to think, I know better
now), and as the sun went down she closed
her eyes, and went to her mother. We buried
her in the little enclosure which we Cetara
fishermen had made for those we loved, and
which had been consecrated by the priest.
We put the flowers that Mariti loved best on
the grave, and a cross over it, and then little
Carlotta and I went back to our lonely home.
From that time, until little Carlotta was old
enough to sing in the streets, as her mother
had done, I taught her all I could. She
learned to make the fine nets used in anchovy
fishing, to read, and to pray. We went on
our donkey to the church in Amalfi, on
saints' day, and Mariti was pleased with us
then. Our flowers bloomed, and the sun
shone.

"At last, .Carlotta and I went about as
musicians; I played on the guitar and she
sang. We went to Naples, and twice to
Rome. The strangers called us into the

hotels, and Carlotta sang to them. Once, a beautiful American lady played on the piano while Carlotta sang. We were well known, and well supported. Carlotta was very beautiful, and looked as well as any of the great ladies. She dressed in the holiday suit of the Amalfi women, for I found the strangers thought more of her if she was what they called 'in costume.' Those were happy days. Mariti was pleased, and every day, as we went out in the bright sunshine, I thought she made it light for us. I did not know then about the Saviour; I thought Mariti was a saint, and took care of me. I used to pray to her; I am sure she was as good as the saints I heard about in those days. Often, in Rome, Carlotta and I would go into the churches for our morning prayers, but while she prayed to Holy Maria, I prayed to Mariti. I hope I am forgiven for that sin.

"We lived in this way for several years. We often went back to Cetara, and tried fishing again. Carlotta liked to go with me at night,

when we had the torches lighted on floats
to attract the fish ; she would keep as still as
any of the men while we surrounded the fish
that came in shoals to the lights.   We had to
row very quietly, and to get our nets around
them ; then suddenly we put out the lights,
beat on the water with our oars, and drew in
the nets full of the frightened little fish
Carlotta screamed with delight when our net
was full, and then she would cry to have
them thrown back into the water.   Sometimes I threw them back to please her, for I
remembered that when I was first married,
Mariti made me do the same thing.   The
Cetara fishermen laughed at me, and said it
was better for them, as the fish swam again
after their light, but Carlotta never would
believe that they were caught again.   Those
were happy times : Mariti was pleased with
me then, the flowers bloomed and the sun
shone.

"One bright, spring day, in Rome, when
the young leaves were coming out, and the

birds were singing, Carlotta and I were passing through the Piazza del Popolo, and stopped to rest by the fountain at the foot of the obelisk. I thought I had never seen any picture so beautiful as my grand-child—except Mariti! Mariti, my saint! Her eyes were bright, and yet soft and dreamy; her hair was black and glossy, her complexion was a clear olive, with a healthy color, coming and going with every changing thought; the brilliant hues of her dress heightened her beauty. I stood before her as she half reclined on the marble steps, and I asked Mariti to let me keep my grand-child. Mariti could not have heard me that day. What was I, that she should always be ready to listen? Oh, I forget, I am talking as I thought then. Since I have known my Saviour's love, I have asked Him to forgive me for praying to one who had no power to help me, but I knew no better then, and I am old now, and get confused as I go back to the old days.

"We staid a long time by the fountain, till I

was attracted by the wandering of my little
girl's eyes. Instead of their laughing back
replies to my words, they looked behind me
at a young man, who was walking about,
pretending to be much interested in the
obelisk, but who, alas! was looking at Carlotta.

"I found that he could see beauty in my
little girl as well as I. He asked me some
civil question about the obelisk, but I was
angry, and did not reply, but called her to
come away, it was time to come home.

"She said nothing as she walked by my side,
and the next songs she sang were sad love-
songs, and—but I do not like to go back to
that day—I felt I had lost my grand-child,
and—that—Mariti—had not heard my prayer!

"The young man, an American, followed
her around, told her wonderful stories of his
country, said if she would marry him and go
there, she need never sing in the streets any
more, and that I should go too, and, finally,
with his soft voice and loving ways, he per-

suaded her to be his wife. They were married
in Amalfi, where Mariti and I were married,
but Mariti did not seem pleased with me, and
yet I could not help it.

"There were no happy days for me then.
John Wilson was the name of my grand-
daughter's husband : he had been employed as
a sort of courier by an American family. He
talked a little French and very good Italian,
but did not know enough of the ways of our
people to manage their affairs, so they paid
him well and dismissed him. When we met
him, they ha l one to Germany, and he was
preparing to go home. Carlotta did not want
to go to America ; so to please her he tried to
get employment in Naples and Sorento, while
Carlotta stayed with me in Cetara, for he
would not let her sing any more. She was
not happy away from him, and, finally, I told
her she had better go to Naples and stay with
him, while I continued my old life of fishing for
anchovies at Cetara.

"It was a sad day when she left me, but I

did right to send the child to her husband,
and Mariti was pleased with me. I passed
two very lonely years, but saved up a little
money for my old age, for I knew the time
would come when I would be too old to fish.
During these two years, I saw Carlotta several
times at Castel e Mare, where we agreed to
meet, and the last time we met there, she
told me that her husband was determined to
go to America; that she had told him she
could not go and leave me. He said I might
go, and he would pay my way over the ocean,
but then I must support myself there. I asked
her how? She said that John told her that
there were places in New York where I could
hire an organ and a monkey, and go around
the streets and get money. She said to him
if she had a little girl to go round with me it
would do very well, but she did not like me
to go alone. John told her nothing would
hurt me, and that no child of his should go
around the streets for money. I told her I
would rather fish in Cetara.

"'But *I* must go,' she said. 'Oh, father, do try it. John has a plan about a little girl. I am sure you will not be lonely, he will let **you** come home to me every night.'

"'What do you mean about a little girl?' I asked.

"She did not tell me very plainly, but seemed confused, and said I must sell everything in Cetara and come to her in Naples, and she would tell me.

"I finally promised to do so, and went back to Cetara. I went to the old church in Amalfi again, and prayed to Mariti, but she did not seem pleased. I hope my Saviour has forgiven my prayers to my wife,—the only saint I really cared for. I was afraid to go to Naples after this, but I had a letter from John, telling me that he would make it all plain for me, and that he had taken passage for America. I wanted so much to be with Carlotta, that I sold out in Cetara, and joined John and Carlotta in Naples. I did not tell them how much money I had saved up, for I thought I might

grow too old to carry an organ, and then I
would want my money in the strange land of
America. Now, I must tell you the wicked
part of my story, and that I never dared to
pray to Mariti any more. She never was
pleased with me again for a long time.

" John said he knew a child, belonging to an
English family who had gone off to Russia,
and left it in Naples under the care of a nurse.
He said the nurse was very careless about the
child, and he thought we had better take it
with us to America. Carlotta would be very
kind to it, and could bring it up to go about
with me, and have the same happy life she
used to have. I turned pale with horror.
Though I knew children were stolen sometimes, I had no wish to do such wickedness.
John had a very persuasive way, and, after a
long time, he made me see how much better
it would be for the child than to be so badly
treated by its nurse, and perhaps forgotten by
its parents. I would not help to do it, for
when I felt that I dared not tell Mariti, I

knew it was wrong. You see, in my ignorance, I made Mariti a sort of a god. I know better now, and I hope I am forgiven.

"One afternoon Carlotta dressed herself in a Roman dress, and went out to sing. She was frightened and her eyes were red, but she did not tell me why she was going to sing again. John went out too. They told me afterwards what they did. John had become acquainted with the English nurse, and he made.believe that he was in love with her. She did not know about him, for whenever he talked to her he wore a Neapolitan dress, and talked broken English. She thought he was an Italian. On this day, she was walking, as usual, in the Villa Reale with the child. John spoke to her, and persuaded her to listen to his foolish talk and love-speeches, until she forgot all about the poor baby, who wandered off near Carlotta. She enticed it away, and, watching her opportunity, took it into one of those little shops where lava ornaments are sold. There was a back door to that shop which communicated with the garden of the house where we lived.

"The baby was a good little thing, about two years old, and seemed much pleased. I was so frightened when Carlotta came in with it that I could not speak, but sat, in a dazed way, looking at Carlotta and the woman who kept the lava shop.   They gave the child something to make it sleep, then undressed it, burned its clothes, and stained it all over with something that turned it brown ; they cut off its long, beautiful, golden curls, and washed its hair with something that made it black.   They burned up the curls—all but one, which I saved.   Here it is a mass of gold threads.   She never knew I had it. Soon John came in, and said the nurse had been distracted at the loss of the child, and had gone directly to the English minister, that he had pretended to give her all the help he could, but had put her on the wrong track, by showing her a boat which was, for some unknown reason rowing with all speed

out of the bay. 'Destroy everything,' he
said ; 'they will never know that little brown
child, it is yours now, Carlotta.'

" The Roman dress was burned too, and no
sign remained of the fair and beautiful English
child.   The whole foreign population of Naples
were seeking for the child, advertised as
'very fair, with dark eyes, and a profusion of
golden curls.' In the midst of the excitement,
Carlotta, with her brown, short-haired child,
and old grandfather, sailed for Marseilles,
where John promised to meet us soon after
our arrival.

" The whole thing was done so suddenly
and so successfully that I had no power to
remonstrate or to regret : I only hoped Mariti
did not know.   Whatever I ventured to say,
was answered by, 'See how happy see is.   I
will take good care of her.'   I grew accustomed to it after a while.   We met John at
Marseilles, and from there sailed to America.
We took good care of the child, and she was
soon able to go with me with the organ and

monkey. I bought one of my own, and made
a pretty good support. Sorella was the happiest child in the world, and loved Jocko and
her wandering life, better than she ever did
her nurse and her fine clothes. At last, John
and Carlotta decided to go to the western
country, and I was to be left alone. Carlotta
wanted to take Sorella with her, and yet did
not wish me to be alone. It nearly broke her
heart, but John did not give her much time
to think about it ; he was in a great hurry to
get off, and said Sorella should stay with me.
She was nearly seven years old then, and
had been with us five years. John promised
Carlotta, that as soon as they had a comfortable home of their own, they would send for
us. He told me he would write to me ; that I
must not write to either of them ; that he was
going to change his name, so that their knowledge of the child could not be traced. He
would not tell me his new name, and I have
only heard once from them since they left,
which was a year ago. The one letter I

received, was left at the door by a strange man, and only said 'All well,' and enclosed fifty dollars. John was very kind about money. We always had what we needed, and before he went away he gave me a year's board. I have taken good care of Sorella. She has been kept clean and comfortable. If she does not know much, she knows no evil; she has never left me, so she has no bad habits and knows no bad words. There was but little I could teach her. When we have not been wandering about, we had a good room to live in, and were very happy together. My organ has seemed too heavy lately, and I knew this would be my last journey.

"I thank you all for your great kindness in taking care of us. Sorella has been very happy here. I am glad you let her keep Jocko; he is a good little fellow, and has earned many a penny for us. He is not a common monkey. The man I bought him of paid a great price for him. He was saved from a museum which had been burned out. He let me have him at a low price because he was going away, and Sorella got to be so fond of him I kept him for her. Do not take Sorella away while I live. Soon I shall die and go to Mariti. If you can restore her to her parents, without doing any harm to John or Carlotta, I hope you will do so. My money is nearly spent. I am very thankful I came here. I want to say 'thankful to Mariti,' but the good lady has taught me about One who is greater and better than Mariti. I trust in Him, and pray to Him now. Mariti used to talk to me about Holy Maria's Holy Son. Mariti knew all that was good. I can say no more now."

All this long story Mr. Montgomerie wrote down as Mrs. Montgomerie translated it. Mariano was very weak, and had to rest many times, and take refreshments to keep up his strength. When he had finished, he sank back on his pillow. Sorella came in, and with Jocko, nestled down beside him. A look of calm repose came on his face, which had before worn a troubled look. He laid his hand on Sorella's head and quietly slept.

XIV.

Sorella Goes to Burnside.

NOT many days after this, the old organ-grinder died.   His funeral was at the Mission Chapel. They had the beautiful Church Service, and the choir. of children to sing the hymn, beginning :

" Thou art the way,. to Thee alone."

A few words were said in regard to Mariano's early life, his faithful fulfilment of all his known duties, and his final trust in his Saviour.   The older members of the Montgomerie family, Miss Sables, and several other friends, with Sorella and Jocko hugged tight in her arms, followed the body to the grave.   Grandma said, that for Mariti's sake, he should not have a pauper's funeral.

When all was over, Sorella, Jocko, and their few possessions were taken to Burnside, there to remain until Sorella could be restored to her parents. This, it was thought, could be done through the English minister who was resident at Naples at the time that Sorella was stolen. Mr. Montgomerie wrote to him, stating such facts as were necessary, without mentioning the part played by Carlotta and John. It must be some time before an answer could be received, and grandma hoped to get Sorella's hair and complexion in order, so that there might be some hope of her being recognized by her parents; there being no other proof of the truth of the old man's story. The curl was carefully preserved, but every article of clothing which she had on when stolen, had been destroyed.

Sorella was a gentle child, easily governed, but it seemed hard to gain her affections. She had loved her grandfather (as she always called him), with a strange, wild devotion; but she expressed little feeling at the time of his death, and none for any one else, and until they were in the carriage to go to Burnside, Mrs. Montgomerie was doubtful whether the lonely little creature understood that she would see him no more. In the carriage, she attempted to talk to poor Sorella, but the child lifted up a tear-stained face, gave one scream, and fainted.

Mrs. Montgomerie was quite unprepared for this, but it showed that there was deep feeling within the young heart, although outwardly Sorella had been so calm. She took the little one in her arms, and held her lovingly until they reached Burnside. John took her from his mistress, and laid her on the sofa in Mrs. Montgomerie's room. Jocko looked melancholy enough, but managed to scramble upstairs after them, taking no notice of Polly's low-toned " S'cat," or of Jip's advances toward friendship. He climbed up on the bed and gazed in the face of his little mistress with a look of despair. Grandma patted the poor little fellow, for her heart had room enough even for a

monkey, and as Sorella revived, moved away,
leaving Jocko to be the first object on which
the eyes of the little girl rested.

"Poor Jocko," whispered Sorella, "we must
try to be good children, grandfather said so.
Jocko, do you hear?" Then she put out her
little hand to grandma, and said, "Thank you
ma'am; please forgive me for doing so, I
didn't mean to be naughty."

"My darling little girl," exclaimed grandma,
pleased with this expression of feeling, "you
are not naughty, you may do just as you feel.
I know you are very sad, but I will love you
now, my dear little one; and you and I will
talk about grandfather, and you shall try to
do just what he told you."

This seemed to comfort Sorella, but she
only said, "Thank you ma'am," and then
closed her eyes, and fell asleep.

Grandma watched beside her, thinking what
a strange charge had been given to her, and
wondering whether the little one would indeed find a mother's and father's love await-

ing her.   She was not sure what Sorella knew
about her probable future life, and determined
to say nothing to her, until some answer was
received from Naples.

When Sorella waked, she was well enough to
get up and be dressed for dinner.   The little
room next to grandma's was prepared for her,
and new clothes waiting, and grandma's own
maid, Susan, ready to attend to her.   Everything had been done to place her in the
position from which Mariano Zachiti thought
she had been taken.   The dye on her face was
wearing off very rapidly.   Her hair had been
cut short, so that the reddish black had all
disappeared.   Soft, brown hair was growing
in its place, and when dressed, she was
almost pretty.   She expressed no surprise,
but took every change in her usual quiet
way.

She asked if Jocko could go to dinner with
her, and when she had permission to take
him, she washed his face, brushed him carefully, and with a painful stillness, so unlike a

child, she went down-stairs with her odd little pet.

Grandma made the dinner very pleasant, talking in a quiet, but cheerful way of her surroundings, encouraging Sorella to talk, and enjoying with her Jocko's oddities.

After the dessert had been put on the table, and John had gone, grandma saw a pale weariness coming over the little girl, and without remarking upon it, she said :

" Come, dear, let us take our plates of nuts, and sit by the fire. You may have this nice arm-chair, and put your feet on this little foot-stool. Let Jocko sit beside you. There, now you can rest, and I will feed you and Jocko, too."

So grandma drew her chair close beside them, and amused herself very much with the monkey and the nuts, letting Sorella look on without speaking, until the color began to return to the tired little face. A slight noise at the door made them both turn. Polly was standing there, uncertain whether or not to come in.

"Grandma," said she, in a low voice, "S'cat."

"Come in, Polly," said grandma. "Jocko will not hurt you."

Polly walked slowly around in a very side-wise fashion, keeping her eyes on Jocko, and making a very wide circle, before she would perch on grandma's shoulder.

Jocko did not offer to hurt her, so that Polly began to talk in her usual manner. Sorella very nearly laughed, but seemed so weary with everything, that grandma concluded to let her take another nap.

"Come, Polly, I am going up-stairs. We will leave Sorella and Jocko till tea time. Then, Sorella dear," said she, turning to her, "you and I will have a little more talk. Now you may lie down on the sofa, and no one will disturb you for a long time."

Sorella thanked her very quietly, and Mrs. Montgomerie went away with Polly.

If Mrs. Montgomerie had listened at the door, which she did *not* do, she would have heard Sorella say :

"Oh, Jocko, I'm *so* tired, *so* tired of everything. I wonder what I am, and where I am going! Why are they so kind? Are we to live here, Jocko? Shall we never go rambling round the country again, you and grandfather and I? Will God take good care of grandfather? How will he live without his little girl? Oh, Jocko, Jocko, it's very hard." And then she buried her head in the sofa cushions, the tears rolling down her cheeks, and with Jocko's little soft head close beside her, she slept for sorrow.

As grandma knew, for she knew all about sickness and sorrow as well as about joy and happiness, Sorella's heart was very sad. Her days of anxiety had wearied her, her grandfather's death had shocked her whole nervous system, (as the doctors call the part of us that aches), and she needed rest and quiet, more than amusement.

The little girl was in a true home, where love and tenderness would guard her from

care, until she was able to resume her own
duties again.

After some hours, Jocko became rather tired
of so much resting, and as his little mistress
was still asleep, he slid down from the sofa,
crept through the space where grandma had
opened the door a little while before, and began a journey round the house. Everything
was still ; Jocko crept about the hall, climbed
on the hat-stand, examined Polly's cage, which
was empty, and tried to get in it. Helped
himself to her sugar and apple ; then went to
the library, and finding grandma's desk, where
he had seen her write, took her pen, dipped
the handle in the ink, and put it in his mouth.
Not liking the taste, he wiped it on the crimson cloth, and then put it in a vase of flowers,
which he stirred with the pen, until the water
was black, and the flowers stirred out on the
table. After this, he mounted on the piano,
tore a paper lamp shade, in trying to get it on
his head, which having done, he began to
walk up and down the keys, at first very

gently, then perhaps reminded of the old organ, he began to dance, and was having a delightful time, when Mrs. Montgomerie hearing the piano, and supposing it was Sorella, sent Susan to the library, to say that she would be down in a few minutes.

Susan reached the door, just in time to see the last of Jocko's dance, and the remnants of the lamp-shade fall on the floor. At that moment he discovered a pair of spectacles, which he put on, and taking a book began chattering and making gestures. Susan stood in helpless despair, while Jocko, evidently enjoying the situation, made the most absurd faces at her. The piano had wakened Sorella. Missing Jocko, she ran to find him, and reached the door nearly as soon as Susan.

Jocko screamed with dismay the moment he saw his little mistress, dropped everything, and ran up the curtain, on which he left the mark of his inky paws, scrambled from the cornice to the top of the door over Sorella's

Bright…

head, out into the hall, made one jump for
Polly's cage, and squeezed himself into it.
Mrs. Montgomerie had come down in the
midst of the confusion, and taking in the
whole affair at a glance, threw herself on the
sofa to laugh. For added to it all was Polly's
consternation. She had been put, as usual, on
the hat-stand, and was slowly making her way
to her cage when Jocko dove into it, chattering and grimacing in the wildest monkey
fashion. Polly stood perfectly still, words
evidently being utterly inadequate to express
her indignation. Sorella, just roused from
sleep, looked rather bewildered, and could only
exclaim :

"Jocko ! Jocko ! You naughty, naughty
Jocko ! What have you done ? I ought to
have tied you to my arm."

"Take him out, my dear," said grandma,
still laughing, "and come see his work."

Sorella took Jocko out, he scolding and
resisting. She sat down on the floor, stood
him up before her, and very decidedly boxed

14

his funny little ears, saying : "Jocko, bad monkey, bad monkey."

Jocko understood, and looked very sorry. Sorella would not forgive him so soon, but tied him to a chair with a string only long enough for him to clamber on its back, and then began to remedy the disorder of the library.

"Please forgive him," she said ; "he always wants to examine a new place, and I ought to have tied him. I can mend the lampshade, but oh, the ink ! Dear madam, what shall I do ?"

"Nothing, dear Sorella, there is no evil great unless it cannot be remedied. We can take out the ink spots, and I would not have missed this scene for twice the disorder." And grandma laughed so heartily that Sorella's anxious look vanished ; but she gathered the flowers, washed the vase, and replaced them, with quiet care.

After tea, grandma, having noticed how bright Sorella looked as she tried to restore the effects of Jocko's mischief, said :

"Will you do something for me to-morrow, Sorella?"

"I will be very glad to do *anything* for you, ma'am," replied Sorella, earnestly.

"Thank you, dear. I want you to feed the little snow-birds for me every morning after our breakfast. There is a board at the foot of the steps of the east piazza, which John sweeps off very carefully. On that about fifty little birds come for their breakfast, and when the warm sun shines on them, they hop and jump about as merrily as in summer."

"Are they all alike?" asked Sorella, much interested.

"No, some of them are what are called snow-birds, one or two robins, some sparrows, or what the country people call chipping birds, and blue birds. I wish you would count the different kinds, and tell me when there is a new one. I want to find out what kinds of birds can live through our winters. It will help me very much, dear, if I can depend upon you to be faithful, for the bird breakfast is what I never neglect, and yet it is at a very inconvenient hour. What can you do with Jocko, then?"

"I will fasten him somewhere. I have a chain and padlock for him. It is the only thing he cannot undo, and you *may* depend upon me, I will not forget. Please trust me," answered Sorella.

"I will trust you, dear," replied grandma.

Sorella's education had begun.

The little girl looked thoughtful a moment, and then said:

"When Carlotta went away, she said, 'Sorella, promise never to leave grandfather. No matter where you go; take care of him, he is good, and kind, and true. I trust him to you.' I took all the care of him I could, didn't I, ma'am?"

"You certainly did, my child, and now he does not need your care, he has all he wants. You may be happy in thinking about him."

"I don't think he could be happy without Mariti. Is she there, too?" asked Sorella.

"My dear little girl," replied grandma, "whoever believes and trusts in our Saviour will be received and taken care of by Him, when they leave this world. From what Mariano used to say of Mariti, I think she did love her Saviour. She may not have understood all that we do about Him, but He would not ask of her what she had no means of knowing. He asks us to *trust* Him, and He never forgets."

"I like that," said Sorella.

"There was a great king, a long time ago, who had very troublesome people to govern, and used almost to despair of ever teaching them to do right. Then he had very troublesome children, who gave him great sorrow, and besides all his cares for others, he did some very wrong things himself, and they gave him more sorrow than anything else, because he really loved God, and was grieved when he broke His laws. Whenever he was in trouble he prayed for help, and he always was helped, and showed how to do right, so that at last he was perfectly sure that the Lord would help all who called upon Him. He wrote a great many beautiful verses about the goodness of the Lord, and one of them I would like you to learn. It is this:

" 'Commit thy way unto the Lord : trust also in Him ; and He shall bring it to pass.' "

Sorella learned it very readily, and said : " How good that is ! but—" she hesitated, " I like to help myself, too."

" The same king wrote," replied grandma, " 'Trust in the Lord and do good.' You may trust and work too."

" Thank you, that is better still, I like to trust you, dear madam, but I like to do things for you, too," answered the little girl.

Mrs. Montgomerie kissed her, and said : " Now, let us go and put Jip to bed. Then we will sing a hymn, and go ourselves, for it is very late. You took such a long nap that it was nearly nine o'clock before we had tea."

Sorella took her hand confidingly, and they went together to make Jip comfortable. As

they passed, Polly sleepily said, "Go to bed,
go to bed." And Jip, curling himself up in a
little black knot, licked the hand of his mistress as long as he could reach it. Then they
went to Mrs. Montgomerie's room, and together sang—

> " Father, to Thee my soul I lift,
>   On Thee my hope depends,
>   Convinced that every perfect gift
>   From Thee alone descends.
>
> " Mercy and grace are Thine alone,
>   And power and wisdom too ;
>   Without the Spirit of Thy Son,
>   We nothing good can do."

Sorella could understand these simple words,
and even though she was such a little girl, she
trusted her Father in Heaven to take care of
her, and slept in peace.

XV.

About the Snow-birds and the Snow-white Swan.

THE next morning Sorella was brighter and stronger. As soon as breakfast was over, Jocko was fastened to a pillar on the front piazza, which was partly in sunshine, while Sorella attended to the bird breakfast.

The little girl was delighted with the numbers and varieties of birds that came, and vainly tried to count them. They hopped on and off the board, and, as she afterwards said, "they twinkled so," that counting was impossible. After the little birds were satisfied, some beautiful pigeons, that lived at the stable, came for their breakfast, and soon ate all that was left. Sorella came in with quite a bright color, and began to tell grandma about it, when she heard a tapping at the window. There was little Jocko, rather tired of being alone, and perhaps a little cold, trying to make his mistress attend to him. This she did at once, and as she brought him in, Polly ventured to say, quite loudly, "So ho, sir, come in, 'hollo Jock—o !"

Jocko made a very funny face at her, at which Polly said "S'cat," as usual when she did not feel entirely pleased. Jocko, who preferred Polly's cage to Polly's self, took no farther notice of her, and Sorella, seeing grandma seated quietly in the library, found a footstool and sat beside her.

For a while the birds, their habits, and the habits of pet animals formed a pleasant theme of conversation. Grandma then asked Sorella how she liked her old life with her grandfather.

"Very much, indeed, madam," she replied ; "but better in the country than in the city, for in the city I was afraid of the boys."

" Did the boys ever offer to trouble you ?" asked grandma.

"Not very often, madam, but they said such bad words that it frightened me to hear them. Grandfather said I must be like a swan's back," said Sorella.

" My dear, I do not understand," said grandma.

" It's like a little story, madam. May I tell you ?" answered Sorella.

" Certainly, my child, and I think you had better call me grandma, then you will love me better." This was said with such a kind look, that Sorella thought that she loved Mrs. Montgomerie very much already.

" Thank you, ma'am; and if my story tires you, please tell me.

" Grandfather said that once Mariti did some sewing for a noble Roman family ; they were not living in Rome at the time, but were at their country place, the Villa Pamfili Doria. I know the name, because he told me so often. He and Mariti were in Rome, and

had to take the work out to the villa.   So
one beautiful morning, while the dew was
still on the grass, they got on a little donkey,
both of them, ma'am, and trotted out of the
Porta San Pancrazio, along the road to the villa.
It was early in June (I believe, ma'am, the
family only lived at their country home in
May and June, because it was unhealthy after
that), everything was very beautiful, and as
the sun rose behind them it shone on the
dew-drops, and Mariti laughed and sang with
happiness as she saw the glistening leaves and
shining rose-buds.   It was a very happy ride.
Soon they reached the gate of the villa, and
the little donkey trotted on over the smooth
roads.   Mariti said : 'Mariano, it is too early
to see the Princess Doria's maid, let us tie
the donkey and walk about.'   So they tied the
little donkey and had a beautiful walk about
the grounds.   Among other beautiful things
they saw, was a pond with a fountain in the
centre, and floating about on the pond a
beautiful white swan.   He curved his long

neck back when he saw them, and floated to where they were, to see if they had anything to give him. Mariti had some biscuit, which she threw on the water. Grandfather said her little hands tightened on his arm with her delight at seeing this lovely creature."

Sorella stopped, with tears in her eyes. She had repeated the whole account as if she had learned it, and grandma said : " Rest a moment, my dear child. What a picture it is, of Mariano and his beautiful wife, standing beside the pond, in those lovely grounds. I have been there, Sorella, and have stood in that very place."

" Oh, did you see the swan, ma'am ?" exclaimed Sorella.

" I cannot say whether I saw the same one, but I certainly saw the most beautiful swan there that I ever could have imagined. His mate had just died, and he was floating about in a very sad, lonely way," she replied.

" Grandfather only spoke of one. Shall I

go on, grandma ?" asked Sorella, hesitating a
little as she said " grandma."

" Yes, dear, I enjoy your story very
much."

" Then grandfather said : 'Sing to him,
Mariti.' So she trilled out some bird-like song,
and the swan laid his proud head back to listen.
Then he floated up under the fountain and
let the diamond drops fall upon his snow-
white feathers. Each one rolled down, and fell
off into the crystal water ; his feathers were
not even wet, but were as pure and as undis-
turbed as before. Mariti raised her face,
bright with a new thought : ' Mariano,' she
said, ' when our hearts are pure and beautiful
nothing will disturb them. Evil, though it
may touch us, will roll off without ruffling a
feather.'

" ' Like your own sweet heart, my Mariti,'
he answered.

" ' No, Mariano, not that, but like every
heart our Lord has made pure.'

" The gardener came to them then, and

they were taken into the servants' hall, and had bread and fruit given them, while they waited for orders about work.

"As they went home on the little donkey, they met a man saying evil words to induce his overladen animal to go faster. Mariano spoke to him about it, but it made him worse. 'Come away,' said Mariti, 'do not listen to him, and let the memory of his words roll off, as the drops from the swan.'

"Then grandfather always cried, and said: 'This was Mariti, my saint. Do you wonder that I loved her?' Oh, madam, it was beautiful to live with grandfather."

"My dear, he certainly was a very interesting old man; the more I knew him, during his life, the better I liked him, and the more I hear of him, the better I respect and love his character. Do you remember where you lived when you were in New York?" asked Mrs. Montgomerie.

"Yes, ma'am, I remember it very well. We lived with an Englishwoman, Mrs. Martin. It

was in a broad street, with a railway in it.
Mrs. Martin called it Hay Havenue."

"Do you think it was Avenue A ; she might
have pronounced it in that manner ?" asked
Mrs. Montgomerie.

"No ma'am, it was an avenue with a number, and we lived opposite a large house,
that grandfather said the Protestants had
built to hold a very large Bible, that they
thought a great deal of," returned Sorella.

Mrs. Montgomerie was rather bewildered
by Hay Havenue, and an avenue with a number, and the large Bible, but suddenly a
gleam of light came on the subject, and she
asked : "Did you live opposite to the Bible
House, on Third Avenue ?"

"Oh, yes, ma'am, that was it.   The house
for the Bible, but it was Fourth Avenue, not
Third," she answered, eagerly.

"But what was Hay Havenue.   Why did
Mrs. Martin call it that ?"

"She was very proud of it, grandma, and
said she ought to ask more for her rooms,

because they were on Hay Havenue, instead of a cross street."

"Oh, I understand," said Mrs. Montgomerie, with one of her merry laughs; "but did Mariano really think that building was to contain one book?"

"Yes, ma'am, he often told me so. He thought so, or he would not have said so. He tried to explain to me about the Protestant Bible, for he said I ought to be a Protestant, and I think Mrs. Martin could have told me about it, but grandfather never let me see her unless he was there. He said she had foolish ideas, and did not speak good English. She was always kind to me, but grandfather said he wanted to teach me himself, and that after he died I could learn other things. He said there were a great many Bibles in this country, but there was one larger than all the rest, and that it was called the Holy Bible, and was kept in that house."

"What an odd idea," said Mrs. Montgomerie. "We call each Bible, a Holy Bible, because it is the holy word of God ; and we have it in every possible size and price, and the Bible House is a place where Bibles are printed, and bound, and sold. The reading is the same in each Bible ; but some persons want large print, and some want small. Some can pay a large price for a handsomely bound Bible, and some want to pay very little. Every kind that is needed can be found at the Bible House. We want every person to have one. But, my dear, what did you learn out of books ?"

"John taught me to read and to spell, and a little about counting. I learned very quickly, because I can remember anything, if I hear it once or twice. Grandfather taught me a great many little stories, like the one I told you. He said, after he died he wanted me to tell my friends about Mariti, and to show them that he only taught me what was good and pure."

"Whom did he mean by your friends ?" asked Mrs. Montgomerie.

15

"After John and Carlotta went to the west, grandfather told me that I was his adopted child, and that when he died, my friends would come for me. That was all he told me, and sometimes I thought maybe you, grandma, were one of them, but I don't know. He said Mariti would make it all right."

"Oh!" exclaimed Mrs. Montgomerie, who was what people call enthusiastic, "I think your grandfather had the most beautiful nature I ever heard of."

"Do you, do you?" exclaimed the usually quiet Sorella, astonishing grandma by a sudden plunge into her arms. "Oh, I'm so glad, I'm so happy. I did so much want you to understand him. Oh, how I do love you for that!"

Jocko mounted the mantleshelf, and made the most extraordinary faces at this unexpected termination of a quiet talk, but Sorella and grandma were fast friends from that moment. There was no more reserve between them.

Farther conversation was prevented by Jocko, who, being attracted by the ticking of the clock, put his paw on the pendulum and stopped it. As it ceased ticking, he made a little angry sound. Sorella sprang towards him, to stop him before he should touch it, but too late. The mischief was done, and Jocko knowing he had done wrong, was on the cornice in a moment, making such comical grimaces, that grandma could do nothing but laugh.

"But, dear grandma," said Sorella, "what *shall* I do with him? He has done so much mischief already, that I am really unhappy about it. Shall I give him away?"

"No, indeed," replied Mrs. Montgomerie, rearranging the pendulum, and setting the clock. "We will educate him. He is too amusing to part with. Oh, look at him now!"

Jocko was holding by one paw and swinging backwards and forwards with the regularity of the clock's ticking, and seemed as much engaged as if it were his duty to keep time.

Their laughter roused Polly, whose cage being generally open, she had no difficulty in putting her head in the door. At first she did not see the swinging monkey, and joining in the laugh, in her usual way, was coming in, when she suddenly discovered him. "S'cat!" she exclaimed, turning quickly. "Hollo Jocko, S'cat," and trotted back again as fast as possible, getting into her cage with all speed.

"Our pets will keep us employed," laughingly said grandma. "Get Jocko down, for we must have lunch, and then we will drive to the village. I have calls to make, and would like you to amuse Nora Herndon for a while. She is so glad when you can go to her."

"Yes, dear grandma," replied the little girl. "I cannot be very happy, but I will talk to Nora or read to her, if it will do her any good."

"It will, I am sure. Ask Nora to show you her new Bible with pictures, particularly the picture next to the twenty-third psalm, if you can remember it."

"Twenty-third psalm, twenty-third psalm," repeated Sorella.   "I will remember."

When, some time after this, Sorella entered Nora Herndon's little room, Nora exclaimed : "Oh, how glad I am to see you, dear Sorella !"

"Thank you, Nora.   Are you better to-day ?"

"Yes, indeed, I'm better and better every day.   The doctor says, maybe by spring-time I can walk a little again.   If I can only get out to feed my ducks and chickens, I will be so glad."

"I fed the little winter birds, to-day, at Burnside," said Sorella.   "It was lovely to see them take the grain, and look one-sided at me, as they ate it."

"Isn't it nice at Burnside ?" asked Nora.

"It's very nice, and I ought to be very happy.   But, Nora, did you know about grandfather ?"

"Yes, dear, I know.   I'm very sorry for you ; but I think it must be nice for him, it's so different.   I like an organ very much, but heavenly harps must be better."

"I should think so," said Sorella ; "but I can't help missing him.   People may think about him as an organ man, but he was everything to me.   Oh, Nora, he was so good."

"Was he 'good,' before he knew about the Saviour ?   I don't see how that could be."

"Why, Nora, he couldn't know about Him, till somebody told him, but that didn't prevent his being as good as he knew."

"I guess he was like Cornelius, who prayed to God, and did alms, and I suppose God was pleased with him, for He took the trouble to send Peter to tell him about the Saviour," replied Nora.

"Well, it was just the same with grandfather.   God sent Mrs. Montgomerie to tell him about the Saviour, and he took it right in, as if he had been waiting for it.   Oh, Nora,

I was to ask you to show me a picture about the twenty-third psalm." ·

" Here it is, dear, it's lovely, isn't it. See ! there's a shepherd leading that lamb into that lovely place, see 'green pastures and still waters.' Mrs. Montgomerie told me, it's to comfort sick and sorry, and tired people ; to show them how our Lord will lead them into restful feelings."

"I don't know how you mean, about leading into feelings," said Sorella.

" Oh, dear ! I wish you did. I don't know how to tell you exactly, but don't you know how Mrs. Montgomerie does. Maybe she only does so to me ; but some days, when my foot aches all over me, and I can't lie still, and mother is busy, and I feel as if nobody loves me, then she comes in, and I don't tell her how I feel, but she begins such pleasant talk, makes me think how lovely everything is. Tells me about my Saviour knowing all my troubles, and reads some beautiful verses, or tells me some happy thing. I feel as if she led me into feelings that rest me, and always think of green pastures and still waters."

"Oh yes, I know now," said Sorella, "she does just so to me, she don't seem to try, but somehow it's like rain on thirsty flowers, it rests me. Then at other times she is so earnest about things, and it seems so important to do things, that I feel as if I never ought to stop, but *she* knows, she don't do so when I am tired. I love her, don't you?"

"I love her so that it seems as if I never could tell how much, but I only told about her to show how our Saviour—who knows us better than she does—can lead us into quiet, happy feelings. Do you love Him, Sorella?"

"I don't know, I have only heard about Him lately. I think He did a great many kind things, but it was so long ago, and I don't know Him well enough now to *love* Him."

"That's it," said Nora. "It's the knowing Him, that makes us love Him. You didn't love Mrs. Montgomeric till you knew her.

You might have understood all about her goodness, and been willing to trust her to do a great many things for you, but you could not *love* her till you really knew about it all, and till she put her lovely, soft hand on you."

"I know that, but you can't know the Saviour that way. You only hear about Him what some one else says."

"I wish that His hands had been placed on *my* head, that His arms had been put around *me*," sang Nora.

"Well, ye–es," said Sorella, doubtfully, "but that can't be, you know."

"It could have been if I had lived in that lovely time when He was on earth, and His having been here once, makes it easier to know Him now. *I* love Him, I know I do. I tell Him everything, and He hears me. Why, Sorella, that dreadful time when the doctors were hurting my foot so, after it was broken, I asked Him to help me to bear it, and just then one of the doctors whispered to another, "I am sure she can bear chloroform," the other one nodded, and they gave it to me, so that I did not feel any more pain. I know He told them to, because that was the best way to help me."

" But He never did anything like that to me," answered Sorella.

" You don't know that. He brought you here, where your grandfather learned about Him before he died, and maybe some other happy things may come to you because you came here."

" That's a good idea," said Sorella ; " I'll look up the things that happen to me because we came here."

" Then, if they are good things, you'll love Him, wont you ?"

"I don't know," said Sorella. "Suppose they are not good things."

" But, dear, they will turn out good, some-how, if *He* does them."

" Now, Nora, that's where it is, you believe *that* because you love *Him*."

"Sorella, the way to know Him is to read

about Him, to think about Him, to talk about Him. Mrs. Montgomerie told me so. She showed me a place in the Bible where Moses told the Israelites—here it is, I will read it to you. Deuteronomy, eleventh chapter, eighteenth verse—where he told them how to love the Lord and to keep His charge. He first repeated the good things the Lord had done for them, that's in the first part of the chapter, then he said : ' Ye shall lay up these words in your heart, and in your soul, and bind them for a sign upon your hand ; and ye shall teach them to your children, speaking of them when thou sittest in thine house, and when thou walkest by the way, when thou liest down, and when thou risest up.' Now, dear, if you do so about His words, you will soon love Him."

" I will try, dear Nora."

Nora was much older than Sorella, and she knew that it was best not to say any more then, so she talked on some other subject, until the carriage came for Sorella.

Sorella began to know her Saviour on that day, for she seldom forgot anything, and Nora's way of learning about Him was easy to her. She thought of Him, she read about Him, she watched to see whether He heard her prayers, for she prayed to Him now, and before long hoped that she loved Him. She was afraid to be sure that she did, for Sorella was very truthful, even to herself, and she thought if she loved Him as she ought, she would never do wrong.

She was mistaken about that, but if she had thought that if she loved Him she would not *love* to do wrong, that would have been true, and would have comforted her, because she did not love any wrong thing.

She ought to have talked about it to Mrs. Montgomerie, or to some one who could have helped her. But Sorella did not like to talk about herself, and so it was a long time before she had the real comfort of knowing that her heart had turned to her Saviour.

XVI.

About Extra and Minerva.

WHILE grandma was trying to find out how to influence little Sorella, everything was going on at Brightside as happily as ever. Henry and Mary had a new source of interest in Sorella and her fortunes, and every day asked if there had been a letter from Naples. The new rooms were still a great enjoyment, and Mary's doll had been turned into a baby with long clothes, so that she might sleep beside her little mother, in a crib, as babies do. The bedstead which Mary received at Christmas was the crib. The nursery was a delightful play-room, and with Minny's help was kept in very nice order. The children had been early taught to put up one set of playthings, before they took out another, so there was never that hopeless mass of confusion that some play-rooms present. Minny always said : "It's easy 'nuff to do tings when you has de habit of it. Just put dem up *ebery* time and dere wont be no trouble about no tings."

After breakfast, there was usually a visit to .the stable, but so far no signs of the little dogs. Mary said she was afraid they would be so big that she would not know them. They consoled themselves with the pony, who was talked to, and the cow, who was encouraged to hope for spring-time and grass.

"Don't worry about it, Susie," said Henry; "everything comes along, only wait patiently." So Susie ate her hay and waited patiently.

Several hours were spent over lessons, then lunch, and sometimes a drive, either with mamma, or to the village for the French lessons. There was time to play, after their return, before the five o'clock dinner, after which they usually were with papa and mamma until bed-time, which was eight o'clock. Sometimes

they played games, sometimes read, sometimes had music, listening to mamma or singing with her. Sometimes papa and Henry
played charades for mamma and Mary, who
had to guess the words.

One evening they came in and marched
about to represent a band of music, Henry
drummed and papa fifed. Mary guessed that,
exclaiming, " Band, band, I am sure."

The next time they came in, they sang a
love-song, as if they were serenading a lady,but
neither Mary nor mamma could imagine what it
meant.   Then Henry said the next would be
the whole word, and I wish you could have
seen the way papa and Henry changed their
appearance.   They turned their coats inside
out, and bandaged up their heads, put feathers
in their felt hats, which were bent in every
direction, had pistols and swords and carving
knives, and altogether were very dreadful to
look at.   They came in talking about a
carriage which they expected to meet, and
they made their plans to kill the horses and

to rob the people, so that mamma called out "Banditti, banditti." That was right : first band, then the love-song was the ditty, and the whole word was banditti. In such pleasant amusements the hours passed very quickly. Saturday was generally spent at Burnside.

One evening, they were, as usual, in the library. Papa was explaining a puzzle to Henry, mamma and Mary were reading. Mary had the adventures of Alice in Wonderland, and was deeply interested in that charming little book. Suddenly, to the consternation of every one, she burst into a flood of tears.

"My precious child, what is the matter !" exclaimed mamma.

"Oh, mamma, mamma," said Mary, as well as her sobs would allow, "I don't know what extra means, and I never, never shall know ; oh dear, oh dear !"

"My dear child, come to me," said papa, taking her on his knee ; "tell me now, all about it, my poor little philologist."

"Oh, papa, dear, is it anything very bad to be that? I didn't mean to, but I don't understand," said Mary, from under a renewed flood.

"My dear little girl, we must have umbrellas if this is going on," said papa; "a philologist is only somebody who loves to find out everything about words, but I never met one before who cried so much."

"Now, papa, you are laughing at me," replied Mary; "and you don't know how bad it is."

"Try and tell me then," said papa; "how can I learn unless you tell me?"

"Well, papa, I'll try," said Mary: "You see, a long time ago, grandma said Lucy wanted an 'extra' to help her cook the dinner. I thought maybe it was a stove, or a saucepan, but I thought I would ask Minny, because she knows about cooks, and papa"— here the tears came down afresh—"she told me it was clothes, over the usual number, that went to the wash. Only think of it, papa!"

16

"Go on, my darling, I'm beginning to understand," said papa.

"Then another day I asked Henry, and oh, papa, that was worse than ever, he said it was a *railroad train!*" Here Henry laughed heartily.

"Poor little birdie! I'll tell you all about it soon, go on with the story."

"Then, papa,"—and here Mary seemed to wish not to reproach him,—"you, dear papa, I asked *you*, and I don't believe you heard me, for you said—oh! papa—you said it was a *newspaper!*"

"Did I?" said papa; "I ought to have explained it then—any more?"

"Now, papa, I was reading about Alice, and the Mock Turtle asked if she learned extras, and she said: 'Yes, we learned French and music,' and then the Mock Turtle asked if she learned washing, and then I just gave up and cried."

Papa was rather mystified about the Mock Turtle, and said he could explain everything but that, for he never had seen a Mock Turtle, and didn't know that they talked, and if they *did* talk, and if this Mock Turtle was a specimen, they were not very sensible.

"No, papa," said Mary, sadly, "and then they cry so."

"Well, very wise little girls cry too, so we wont blame the Mock Turtle for that. Perhaps he wanted to be a real Turtle," replied papa.

"He was a real one once," said Mary; "but you must read the book, papa."

Papa promised he would : "And now about Extra," said he. "It means anything more than the usual number. It is no particular thing ; only we sometimes say an extra, instead of saying an extra train, or an extra newspaper ; or extras, instead of extra studies at school, or extra articles in the laundry list. Isn't that it, mamma ?"

"Yes, dear," said mamma, giving a very anxious look towards Mary's little tired face ; "and what Lucy wanted was an extra person to help her. Do you quite understand it now, my darling?"

"Oh yes, mamma, now I do. I remember Minny said it was an easy word, and, papa, please tell me about Minny. I asked her why she was called Minny, and she said her name was Minerva, and that the young ladies called her Minerva because her father's name was Jew Peter."

"Indeed!" said papa. "I never heard that classical reason before. Was he the regular old Jupiter?"

"I don't know, papa; he was pretty old, and was the gardener," replied Mary.

"Papa, may I tell you what Minny told us about it?" exclaimed Henry, who had also been much puzzled on this subject.

"Yes, my boy, let us have the whole story."

"Mary asked Minny, and she said she didn't know exactly, but she remembered, when she was very little, that her father told her to dress up fine, for she was to go to wait on the young ladies at the house,—the house where he was gardener, you know, papa."

Papa nodded.

"So she put on a yellow dress, think of it, papa! and had her hair braided all over her head, like little horns. Oh, how she must have looked!"

They all had a hearty laugh at Henry's account, and mamma said she was very glad Minny wore a turban now, for she thought she was very handsome.

"How do you think a helmet would suit her?" asked papa.

"I like a turban better," replied Mary. "Tell them the rest, Harry."

"Then she said she went up to the young ladies' room. They were talking and laughing with their mother, so Minny went quietly in and stood by the door, with her arms behind her back."

"Go on," said papa, "I am ready for the catastrophe."

"Oh, papa, stop laughing. There she

stood without saying a word. Suddenly they saw her. One of them screamed, I think Minny said so, and said, 'What is that?' Then their mother said it must be the little girl to wait on you. 'What's your name, child?' the mother asked (the young ladies' mother, you know, papa). Minny answered : 'I don't know.'—'Who are you?' one of the young ladies asked.—'I'm one of Jupiter's children,' said Minny. Then, Minny says, the ladies all laughed, and one of them said, 'You must be Minerva then, you're such a wise-looking little thing,' so Minny says she was called Minerva ever afterwards."

"Very well told, my boy, and a very amusing account. I had no idea we had such a character in the house, had you, mamma?"

"I always thought Minny was 'wondrous wise,'" said mamma ; "but you must tell the children about Jupiter and Minerva, so that they will understand what we have said."

"Jupiter," said papa, "was the chief of all the heathen gods : I have told you before,

that nations who had forgotten how to worship the true God, worshipped the sun or stars
or great men who had died, and among some
nations almost everything that could be
thought of. You have read in the book of
Acts about Diana of the Ephesians. She was
an object of worship."

"Wasn't it wicked?" asked Mary.

"Very," said papa. "There are people still
who worship false gods, and that is the reason
that we send missionaries to them, that they
may be taught what is truth.

"Jupiter had a great many children. So
those said who worshipped him. One of them
was named Minerva. She was the goddess of
wisdom."

"Is a goddess a lady-god?" asked Henry.

"Yes, Minerva was a daughter of Jupiter.
So as the old gardener's name was Jupiter,
and this little girl was one of his children,
and had a wise look, they called her Minerva.
Do you quite understand about it, my dear
little ones."

Yes, dear papa, quite, and thank you very much for telling us. I'm so glad Minny came here to live," said Henry.

"Now," said mamma, "it is nearly eight o'clock, let us all sing a hymn before you say good-night."

Mary begged for the one about the heathen who bowed down to wood and stone. They therefore united in the familiar words, "From Greenland's icy mountains," and Mary clapped her hands when they came to what she called "the happy part. 'Waft, waft, ye winds, his story, &c.'"

Mamma went up-stairs with them, and before long, these two little children were at rest and asleep.

XVII.

The Little Dogs Again.

A S the family were at breakfast one morning, in the latter part of January, the
waiter brought a message to Master Henry.

"If you please, sir, Tom says the dogs are
found, and if you will go to the stable, after
breakfast, he will show them to you."

The screams of delight interfered greatly
with the proper enjoyment of the buckwheat
cakes. The children knew they could not leave
the table until breakfast was over, but they
thought that one cake was enough for any
one, and Mary could not help saying, "Papa
you are very fond of cakes;" to which papa
composedly said he was "very fond of them,"
and quietly helped himself to more. Mary
sighed, and consoled herself by every sort of

gucss about the size and appearance of the little dogs, now a month old.

Before long they were running down the carriage-path, and calling :

" Tom ! Tom ! where are they ?"

" Up in the little room, Miss Mary," replied Tom. " Tan is dead, miss, and I took thim dogs, and made a bed for 'em in the little room."

" Oh dear, is Tan dead ? What died her, Tom ?" asked Mary.

" Why, miss, you see," said Tom, looking a little uneasy, " sure she drank too much water, and it kilt her entirely."

" Oh, Tom !" exclaimed Henry, " how could you be so careless. She must have got at the horse bucket. Poor little Tan."

" No, sir," said Tom, " it was water from the pond. It was purty cold, too, and it's onhealthy to drink too much cold water."

The children gave up the cause of Tan's death in the delight of seeing the four bright, merry little dogs running round the room, apparently examining their new quarters.

Carlo was the largest and brightest, and seemed to take care of all the rest.

"Oh, Mary ! Mary !" screamed Henry, "see Carlo, he is brushing his brothers and sisters up in a corner and sitting on them !"

" Sure he's a knowing dog," said Tom ; " he is fearful of you, sir."

Carlo evidently intended protection, for he barked with the funniest little baby bark, and wrinkled up his forehead, as if the care of the family was too much for him.   It certainly was more than he could do as the family would not stay behind their big brother—who was just seven inches long, and only " big " in comparison with the others, who were only five.   Mary soon decided the matter by taking the whole family on her lap, where all but Carlo were very contented.   Carlo tried to sit on the floor after the manner of larger dogs, but he was so round, and his fore legs were so short that he was perpetually rolling over.   Then he turned round and barked at the place where he had tried to sit, as if the floor had upset him. Altogether Carlo was a very wonderful dog, and both children thought he was "funnier and cunninger than Jocko." Mary looked suddenly grave in the midst of her joy.

"Harry, they are norphans!"

"What are norphans?" asked Henry, rather doubtfully.

"Why, brother dear, things with no papas or mammas. They only had a mamma, and now she is dead." And the tears came in Mary's eyes.

"Don't cry about it," said Henry; "dogs don't know, and besides there is the bell, it's time for lessons. Come, kiss them good-bye, and let's ask mamma about it."

They bade good-bye, and left Carlo wrinkling his forehead as he tried to sit on his family, fearing they would be carried away by these great giants, as Henry and Mary seemed to these little dogs.

The children ran home; Mary exclaiming, as they entered the hall:

"Oh! papa and mamma, there's been a 'strastrophy down at the stable. Tan is dead, and the dogs are norphans."

"What *do* you mean, my dear little girl?" asked mamma. "What is a ' 'strastrophy' and a ' norphan?' "

"Oh, mamma," said Henry, "she means something that happens, and orphans. Don't you know, mamma? It was Tan's dying; poor little dog, she drank too much water; and now the dogs only have Tom and us."

At this papa laughed so heartily that the children stopped in astonishment.

"My dear children," said papa, "can't you induce grandma to adopt these norphans. She has only a cat with seven kittens, a parrot, two dogs and a monkey; not to speak of Sorella."

"Now, papa, stop, grandma don't want any more. Harry and I will take care of them. They are lovely dogs, and Carlo barks just like a great fierce dog, only it's a little baby bark now. He is too little to go out yet, but you and mamma must come down to see them."

Papa promised. The children went to their lessons, and then Mr. and Mrs. Montgomerie had a hearty laugh over the norphans and their little protectors. Mrs. Montgomerie remembered that a friend of hers was talking about an orphan, a few days before, and that Mary had asked her the meaning of the word, which accounted for her using it upon the first opportunity; and as she very seldom could pronounce a new word correctly, "norphan" was explained. As to "'strastrophy," it must have been from hearing her father say "catastrophe."

"It will all come right, sometime. I have no fear about either of them. The foundations of truth and love are a sure basis for character. Other things will come in time," said papa.

In the afternoon, grandma and Sorella came to dinner; fortunately long enough before dark, for the children to take Sorella to see the dogs. Carlo was still taking care of his "norphans," wrinkling his forehead, and

trying to sit on them. There was great enjoyment in playing with them, as there was
one for each, and Carlo for general superintendent, an office which he filled by perpetually barking at the invasion of his territory.
There were a great many plans made for the
education of the dogs ; and Sorella gave very
superior advice, as she had great experience
in training animals. " They must not be fed,"
she said, " till they will do just what you tell
them. Animals will do anything for food."

" But they would die," said Henry ; "for I
don't think they understand our talk."

" You mustn't mind that," said Sorella.
" A great many monkeys die before they
understand."

"Stop, stop !" said Mary, "they shan't
learn, if they have to die. See how bad Carlo
feels. Come here, you darling, you shan't die
at all."

Carlo only wrinkled the more, and made no
sign of understanding.

Sorella held the saucer of milk, and then

said : "Come, little Carlo, come." At that, the entire family scrambled towards Sorella, and the self-sacrificing Carlo stood aside, as his brothers and sisters plunged their funny little heads into the saucer, spilling nearly all the milk on the floor, then licking each others' heads, while Carlo patiently cleaned the floor.

"Oh dear, dear!" said Mary, "what un-fined recedings. I'm afraid they'll never be teached."

"Of course not," said Sorella. "They had better go to a trainer, if you will not take my advice."

Henry looked rather grave at this, and said he guessed "babies ought to have just what they wanted, it would be time enough to teach them, when they were older."

This consoled Mary, who rubbed a little spot clean on each of their heads, as she said, "for a kissing-place." Carlo barked quite a grown-up bark at this, but Fido and the others took all the chances and changes of their lives with great philosophy.

"Why did not Jocko come?" asked Henry of Sorella.

"He was naughty this morning," replied the young disciplinarian, "and I would not let him leave my room. I locked him in, and grandma hung the key on the hat-stand, in the hall."

"Oh, poor Jocko, wont he be unhappy?' asked Henry.

"That's no matter," said Sorella; "he will get over it, and go to sleep. Wont you show me your pony before we go home?"

Frolic was delighted to have company, and whinnied merrily.

"He says, he is glad to see us," exclaimed Henry; "don't you, Frolic?"

"Hee, he, he, hee," replied Frolic.

"That's the way he says 'yes,'" said Henry.

"It's very like the other thing he said," answered Sorella.

"So it is," said Henry; "and I ought not to be sure about what he says; but I think I can tell. Can't I, Frolic?"

17

".Hee, he, he, hee," said Frolic.

"That's just like the other 'yes,' any way," said Sorella. "Will he eat sugar?"

"Hee, he, he, hee," cried Frolic, very loud indeed, turning his head round to Sorella, who at once gave him one of the lumps which she carried in her pocket to aid in Jocko's education.

"There!" cried Henry, triumphantly, "Frolic meant 'yes,' whatever he said, didn't he?"

Sorella was convinced. Frolic was covered carefully with his blanket, on which was "Frolic" in large red letters on one side, and "Henry" on the other. The children then returned to the house.

After dinner, there was a merry game in the library of what they called "planting," which Sorella soon learned.

"Grandma, you're company," said Mary; "so you must begin."

"If you plant number four, what vine will come up?" asked grandma, at once, for no one ever had to wait for her.

"Oh, that's a hard one," said papa. "Will a four o'clock do?"

"No," said grandma, "not at all."

Papa said he would give it up, when mamma exclaimed "ivy!"

"That's right," said grandma, explaining to the children, that number four was sometimes written IV.

"Yes, in hymns and things, I know," said Mary. "Now, mamma, it's you turn."

"If you plant a toad, what will come up?" asked mamma.

"Is it a tree?" asked Henry.

"No, dear, a vine," replied mamma.

"I know, I know, hops!" exclaimed Henry.

"Right," said mamma. "Now, Henry, it's your turn."

"If you plant the sun, what flower will come up?" asked Henry.

"Sun-flower, of course," said papa.

"No, dear papa, that is a good answer, but not the one I meant," said Henry.

"A rose, then," said papa; "the sun arose, you know."

They all exclaimed, "That will not do at all;" so papa said it was too hard for him, and shrugged his shoulders, in a hopeless way.

"I have it!" exclaimed grandma; "and it is a beautiful one, *morning-glory*, is not that it, Harry?"

Yes, grandma, I'm glad you like it," replied Henry.

They all thought that was the best one that had been given, and Henry said he thought of it in the morning, as he opened his door into the nursery. There was a flood of light pouring into the east window, and Minny, standing looking right at the sun, exclaimed, "See de Glory ob de morning." It was grandma's turn, but she said she wanted Mary to give one for her, so Mary said, "If you plant what papa calls mamma, what tree will come up?"

They all laughed, and papa was required to tell all the names by which he called mamma. Papa said that would be hard to do, as he often made them up to suit circumstance s, but he would try, so he said, as fast as he could speak, " Wify, Lulu, Mamma, Precious, Birdie, Sunbeam, Treasure, Darling, Dear, Pussy, Totty."

" Stop, stop !" cried mamma, " you take my breath away, how can you talk such nonsense. None of those can be planted."

" No, papa, it's not one of all that list.   You call mamma a French name sometimes," said Mary.

" Not Bon soir, or Bon jour, is it ?" asked papa.

" Now, papa, be serious about it, think of something else," said Mary.

Papa pretended to look very grave, and suddenly exclaimed : " I have it, *Chérie*, that's what I call mamma, when I speak in a foreign tongue, but I fail to see what will come up."

Mary looked very wise, but said she could not help any more, and Henry guessed, *Cherry Tree !*

" That's right," said Mary.

" Very good," said papa, " but almost too

difficult for such a matter of fact man as I am. I was a little puzzled with the soft ch of the French, and the hard ch of the English. Now *do somebody* give an easy one."

"Plant fifty thousand, and what tree will come up?" asked mamma.

"That's mathematics," said papa; "I know it's hard, and if it is fifty thousand dollars, I would wish them to come up just as they went down, without turning into trees."

"Now think," said mamma. "Roman numbers."

"More 'foreign tongue,'" said Mary, "and I don't know it at all. It's a grown up one, mamma."

Mamma printed the letters on a paper and showed the children that L stands for fifty, and M for thousand. "Now," said she, "read it."

Sorella read, "L M. Oh, I know, an Elm-tree!" she exclaimed.

That was right, and then grandma said they must go. The carriage came, and with the usual number of kisses and good-byes, and loves to Jocko, and Polly and Jip, they finally were safe in among the blankets and furs, and on their way home.

Henry and Mary were soon planted in their little beds, ready to come up bright and fresh as rose-buds in the morning.

XVIII.

About some Old Friends.

ABOUT a week after this, when Mr.
Montgomerie was in New York attending to some business affairs, he thought it would be well to see Mrs. Martin, and inquire of her about Mariano and Sorella. Grandma had told him what Sorella said of the place where they lived, so that he had no difficulty in finding it.

There was a shop on the first floor, from which he was directed to "go up the back stairs, and knock at the second door on the right."

The knock was answered by a very respectable-looking woman, who said, making a curtsey: "Did you please to want lodgings, sir?"

"No, thank you," said Mr. Montgomerie ; "I wish to see Mrs. Martin."

"I am Mrs. Martin, at your service, sir," she replied, with another curtsey. "Pray be seated, sir."

Mr. Montgomerie took a seat on a very clean, chintz-covered sofa, and Mrs. Martin stood waiting for him to tell his business.

"Sit down, Mrs. Martin. I came to ask whether you ever had, among your lodgers, an Italian organ-grinder and his family ?"

"I had, sir. John Wilson and his wife, her grandfather and a little girl, who called the hold man, grandfather, but I misdoubt whether she was kith or kin to any of them, sir," she answered.

"When did they leave you ?" asked Mr. Montgomerie.

"John and his wife went hoff, sudden-like, more than a year gone by. The hold man and the child went hoff in the hautumn, sir."

"Were they good, well-behaved people ?" asked Mr. Montgomerie.

"I never 'ad no lodgers better than them, sir. John was quick-spoken hat times, sir, but he paid reg'lar, and was sober and honest. The hold man was a simple-'arted hold man, but there wasn't never no fault to find with him, he was partickler like, habout Soreller. I'd 'ave took 'er hout with me on the havenue, and done for 'er, but he wouldn't never 'ear to it, sir," she answered.

"Do you know why John and his wife left here?"

"I can't say, for certain, sir, but I hover-'eard him say to his wife, 'I've seen that nurse in the street again, and I think we 'ad better be hoff.' Then his wife cried a long time, and I went in to see if I could do any-thing for 'er. She said 'no,' that John wanted 'er to go to the West to live, and she did not want to leave the hold man. She never said nothing habout the nurse, and I did not like to hinquire, 'cause hover-'earing isn't always believed in, sir."

"Very true," said Mr. Montgomerie, " and

it is very uncertain also, as one part of a conversation may be heard, and what is most
important left out. How soon did they go?"

"The very next day, sir. And John's wife
cried 'erself hill hat a leaving the hold man,
and begged and prayed me to take care of
him and the child, till such time as they
would send for them, sir. She wanted to
take them with 'er, but John said 'no,' and
she gave up. It was as sorrowful a parting,
sir, as I ever see. The hold man was like one
struck, for days; then he roused up, and went
hoff with his grinder. I never rightly made
him hout, sir, for he was a man of few words,
and his life was bound hup in that child.
They staid nearly a year with me, hoff and
hon, and then, last hautumn, went hoff for a
country journey. I asked where they were
bound. The old man said he did not know,
but Marytee would take care of them. I
never asked who Marytee was, though I hoffin
'eard him speak hof 'er. I thought, maybe,
she was one of them Romish saints, or some

curious creature he worshipped, them for-
eigners has such strange beliefs, sir. I 'ave
been a hoping to see them back again, but
the winter set in, and they 'ave not come.
Pray, sir, do you know habout their where-
abouts? I've been a running hon, and never
hasked."

"Yes," said Mr. Montgomerie, "the old
man is dead, and Sorella is under the care of
my mother."

"Dead, sir! That good hold man! Pray,
if I may be so bold, sir, 'ow did he die? Was
he took suddent, sir?"

"They came into our village in October.
Mariano played on the organ, Jocko danced,
and the little girl took up the pennies : once,
as she went towards him, he put his organ
down on the ground, said,'Sorella, my child,'
and fell in paralysis."

"Oh, dearee! dearee me!" exclaimed Mrs.
Martin.

"He was taken to the Poor House," continued Mr. Montgomerie, "with Sorella and

Jocko, and there he was attended by our own physician, and every possible care taken of him. My mother looks after all the people there, and paid especial attention to him.

"After some time, he recovered sufficiently to give an account of himself. He also received religious instruction, and seemed grateful and happy. Sorella was a great favorite with every one, doing what she could to help others, whenever she could be spared from Mariano, to whom she was devoted. He died in the middle of January, without any suffering, leaving Sorella to our care. The account which he gave us, as far as it relates to his residence here, agrees exactly with what you have told me."

"And Soreller, sir, was she kin to him, sir?" asked Mrs. Martin.

"No, I believe not. Mariano had taken care of her from her childhood, having adopted her, and he wishes now that she should be restored to her relatives," replied Mr. Montgomerie.

"He took good care of 'er, I can testify to that, sir, and I'm glad he did not steal 'er. I always mistrusted habout that child, sir," said Mrs. Martin.

"I think Mariano was free from blame about it, unless he ought to have given information in regard to the child. There will, I hope, be no difficulty in restoring her. If any letters come for Mariano, please send them to my address," said Mr. Montgomerie, writing his name and residence on a card for Mrs. Martin.

"Thank you, sir," replied she. "I am very glad to 'ear habout them, and if Soreller hever wants a friend, I stand ready, sir. There is a few harticles of theirs which I would like you to look hover, sir."

Mr. Montgomerie did so, but there was nothing of sufficient value to take away, so he bade Mrs. Martin "good morning," and left her making deep curtsies.

The next day he returned home, and, after dinner, gave a full account of his visit to Mrs.

Martin, in which Henry and Mary were much
interested. "After that," said he, "as I was
going to the hotel, I met my old friend,
Dorris. Do you remember, mamma, how delightfully they entertained us at Dorris Park,
in England?"

"Indeed I do," she replied; "I hope you
invited him here. Is Mrs. Dorris with him?"

"Yes, to both questions, but I must tell
you all about it. We met in the street, and
walked together; he told me they had only
been a few days in New York, and were at
the St. Nicholas, that his wife was not exactly
an invalid, but was restless and nervous.
Then I said, 'Come directly out to our house,
where she can have quiet and every comfort.'
He thanked me, but said that she was particularly anxious to be in New York, for the
present, but that in the spring they would be
very happy to make us a visit."

"Oh, papa, have they any little girls or
boys?" exclaimed Mary.

"They had one child, I know, and I asked

after it. Dorris said, ' We have lost our little girl,' but in such a sad tone that I turned the subject. As we reached the hotel, he asked me to go in and see his wife, but his manner was so peculiar, so different from the genial, whole-souled Englishman whom I used to know, that I declined then, but said I would call this morning, which I did." Mr. Montgomerie stopped a moment, as if the subject were painful to him, then continued.

"I was taken directly to their parlor—a noisy room, fronting Broadway. Mrs. Dorris was standing looking out of the window, and her husband beside her. They turned as I entered, for by some mistake my card was not taken up. Dorris received me in a constrained manner, which was partly explained by the appearance of his wife, which seemed to keep him anxious, and though she was glad to see me, asked after you, and tried to keep up the conversation, for some reason her mind was in Broadway. She was continually looking out, and forgetting what she had said."

"How did she look?" asked Mrs. Montgomerie.

"She will always be beautiful," he replied; "her eyes are as grand as ever, but her hair is gray, and her face as pale as marble."

"Can it be possible! She used to have such a superb color. There is something strange the matter. Do you think I had better go and see her?" returned Mrs. Montgomerie.

Henry and Mary whispered together, and Henry exclaimed: "Oh! papa, perhaps the little girl they lost is Sorella!"

Mr. Montgomerie started to his feet.

"Harry! Harry! what made you think of that? But I think he meant his little girl was dead—but, oh, my boy, perhaps you are right!"

Mrs. Montgomerie said: "If such could be so, it would explain that anxious gazing into Broadway; but it would be too good to be true! There is something more the matter than the *death* of a child."

"And, mamma," said Henry, "'lost,' don't mean dead, you know."

18

"No, mamma," said Mary, "*I* know that: 'lost' means when you can't find a thing, and dead, means—well—means—not living, you know."

"Dear children," answered mamma, "the word 'lost' does not really mean dead, but it is sometimes so used. Yet it may be that you are right. Papa and I will talk it over, and tell you what we think to-morrow. Goodnight now, my little birds. I would rather you would not speak of this even to our good Minny."

Very devoted kisses were given the children that night, and Mrs. Montgomerie turned pale with the thought of what it would be to lose those little ones.

"I do not wonder at the strange manner and appearance of our friends, if Henry's unexpected idea could, by any possibility, prove correct. What can we do, dear husband, to find out, without raising hopes which may never be realized?" said she, as she returned to the library.

"My dear wife, I hardly know what to say,

or how to act.   Let us, to-night, ask earnestly
for direction from the only safe guide, and to-
morrow we will know what to do.   At present, I am so bewildered by the idea of what
may be in store for my friend, that I am incap-
able of a decision."

The next morning, grandma drove over
early on some charitable errand, leaving
Sorella with Miss Sables.   The whole story
was told to her.

"Oh," said she, "how wonderful that the
way our precious children take to 'words and
their meanings' should have made Henry
think of this.   The word 'lost' was understood by them in its real sense, and may lead
to an early settlement of Sorella's future.   I
want to go directly to New York, to tell
those anxious parents."

" But, mother, we must not raise false hopes.
I propose to write to my old friend, and ask
an explanation in regard to his evident de-
pression.   Then I may find out something
about it," said Mr. Montgomerie.

This was decided upon as the best course to pursue, and there was nothing to be done but to wait for the answer.

The children were in such a state of anxiety, that mamma said they had better not see Sorella until after the answer to papa's letter, as they might accidentally say something about it. They had enough employment with lessons, and the education of the little dogs. There was no starvation system in their teaching, but by holding the little dogs' heads, so that their tongues only reached the milk, Mary soon taught them to eat in a proper manner. Carlo seemed to know what was right without instruction, and became very devoted to Henry, who put him inside of the breast of his overcoat, buttoning it over him, all but his head and fore paws, which stood out in front in a very funny manner.

In this way, he took him up to see papa and mamma, who laughed heartily at his wise look, and wrinkled forehead. Carlo was also introduced to Minny, and the nursery and

little rooms, and was much pleased with every_
thing, particularly the soft mats at the foot of
the mirrors. Mary explained the pictures to
him, tried to make him lie in the doll's bed,
which he would not do, and made him as
happy as possible. It was fully decided that
as soon as he was old enough, he should come
to the house to live.

"It would be cruel to take him from his
family yet," they said ; and this was true,
as his delight in returning to them proved.
He kissed his brothers and sister, and sat
upon them in the most loving manner. The
children left him with great regret, but even if
there had been nothing else to do, it was too
cold to stay very long at the stable.

In a few days a letter was received from Mr.
Dorris. He explained his sadness in a few
words :

"You are right, my friend, a deep sorrow
has befallen us, More than five years ago,
our daughter, Ida, was stolen from the nurse,
under whose charge we had left her in Naples.

"We have sought her in every country in Europe. Finally, my wife determined to try America, and proposed to begin with New York, and as we cannot now advertise or describe our lost child, my poor wife watches at the window, fancying that in the crowded street she may see her pass! Of course, I know the utter hopelessness of our search ; but my wife has revived a little from her deep melancholy, with this new idea, and I do not discourage her. I only pray.

"I trust this will explain all that seemed strange in your old friend,

"ALBERT DORRIS."

The excitement that this letter caused cannot be described. Henry became quite a hero for his suggestion, but caution was still necessary, as Mrs. Dorris was too weak to bear any excitement. While the affair was under discussion, the expected letter came from the English minister at Naples, who had made all inquiries on the subject, stating the

day and date of the loss of the child, and
that the names of the parents were entered
at the Hotel Victoria, Naples, as Mr. and
Mrs. Albert Dorris, Dorris Park, Devonshire,
England; that every effort had been fruitlessly
made to discover the persons who, it was
thought, had stolen her; that this idea had
been given up, and it was now generally supposed that the child was drowned. But the
parents would not believe this, and had gone
to America, in the continuance of their
search.

This decided the matter; there was no
longer any doubt. Henry and Mary were
wild with delight, and talked of Ida Dorris as
freely as of Sorella.

The first thing was to tell Sorella. This
grandma did.

Sorella could only exclaim, " Shall I really
have a father and mother, like Henry and
Mary ?"

"Yes, my darling, a real loving father and
mother," replied grandma.

"But, dear grandma, must I leave *you*? Will they take me away to England?"

"It will certainly separate us, my child; but I hope not immediately, for if we can persuade your parents to remain this year with us, we will do so."

"Dear grandma, I do not know how to bear it. So much has happened to me lately— let me think."

Sorella's thinking ended in the nervous weakness which she had after Mariano's death, and some days passed before it was thought safe to inform her parents. But Mr. Montgomerie wrote at once to Mr. Dorris, telling him that it was a very wise thing to come to America, and that there was very little doubt, that He who over-rules all our lives, would direct their search.

This was rather a blind letter, but encouraged Mrs. Dorris, and filled Mr. Dorris with an indefinable hope that Mr. Montgomerie knew something about it. He thought of it day and night, and, at last, could endure the

suspense no longer ; but, making some excuse to Mrs. Dorris, took the cars, and
reached Brightside, just as Mr. Montgomerie
was going to New York to tell the good news.

How he was told, I must leave till the
next chapter.

XIX.

About Ida Dorris.

MR. Montgomerie knew at once why Mr. Dorris had come. He said :

"Yes, I have good news for you;" and taking him to the library, in a few moments Mr. Dorris was told that Ida lived, was well, and was such a daughter as he might be proud to receive.

"Now, my friend, come and write a telegram to your wife, and by the time dinner is over, Ida will be here."

Mr. Dorris was so overpowered with joy and thankfulness, that he could hardly restrain his feelings. He went to his room, and offered there a heartfelt thanksgiving, after which he carefully worded the following telegram to his wife :

"I have great hope of being, to-morrow, the bearer of good news. You may hope for the best."

He did not dare to say all at once, but intended, after he had seen Ida, to send another.

Mrs. Montgomerie and the children returned from a drive, while Mr. Dorris was in his room. They were soon informed of what had occurred, and Henry and Mary finding papa and mamma too much occupied to talk to them, rushed to Minny with the joyful tidings.

"Oh, Minny! Minny! it's Sorella's real, own father, that has come, and Henry found it out. And her name is Ida Dorris, and—"

"Blessings on de dear child'ns, what's come to dem? Is Sorella's father found real, true, sure nuff?"

"Yes, Minny, yes. Papa was telling us about Mr. Dorris who had lost his little girl, and Henry said, 'Maybe it's Sorella,' and it was that very 'vidual, and here he is. And papa has sent for Sorella and grandma, and help me to dress quick."

"Well, I neber did! Dat's de wonderfullest news. Wont we sing a hallelujah dis night 'bout dat? Why, mas'r Harry, you must gib 'trong tanks dis night, for de blessin' ob helping dat sorrowful father."

At dinner, Mr. Dorris was almost too much overwhelmed with his joy to talk much, but he listened to every word about Ida with deepest interest, encouraging the children to repeat her words and tell of her actions. Mr. Montgomerie had sent to Burnside as soon as Mr. Dorris arrived, thinking it best for grandma and Ida to come over and stay all night, as Mr. Dorris would probably wish to take her at once to her mother.

The message reached Burnside just before dinner. Grandma did not tell Ida (as we must now call her) until she had dined. Then the joyful news was given, and before long they were driving towards Brightside.

There was some trouble about Jocko, whom

it was unsafe to leave, and, under the circumstances, unpleasant to take ; as grandma was
not sure how Mr. Dorris would like to be constantly reminded of his daughter's former life.
Sorella, in her quiet way, decided it by saying :

"Grandma, I have asked John to take care
of Jocko for me till to-morrow. I have
taught Jocko to obey him."

Mrs. Montgomerie said she thought that
was a good idea, being much pleased with her
thoughtfulness.

They reached Brightside about seven o'clock.
Sorella succeeded in appearing composed,
though the brilliancy of her eyes and heightened color, showed her intense feeling. Her
father waited alone in the library for her. No
one witnessed the interview. And an hour
passed (it seemed like three hours to Henry
and Mary) before Mr. Dorris opened the door
into the parlor.

"Come in, dear friends," said he ; "I can
never even express my gratitude to you all.
I have an especial debt,—which I can never

repay—to each one. May it be done to you as you have done to me and mine. My precious child is so wonderfully like her mother that there is no need of any other proof."

Mary whispered to Henry: "It isn't gay enough, it's like school," to which he answered:

"Not a bit, wait a little." In which he was right, for, after these few words, everybody talked together, and said all they wanted to.

Mr. Dorris at once sent another telegram to Mrs. Dorris, whose suspense was almost too hard to bear.

" She is found ; and is all the fondest wishes could desire. We will be at the St. Nicholas, to-morrow, in time for dinner."

After this, they gave themselves up to the enjoyment of the hour. Ida sat close beside her father, saying little, but looking a picture of happiness. The elders talked, while Henry and Mary were not forgotten, but treated as very important actors in the happy scene ; for as Mr. Dorris said, if no letter had been sent from Naples, Henry's thought would have finally restored Ida to them.

Before it was time for the little ones to say "Good-night," Mr. Montgomerie proposed that they should unite in reading the one hundred and third psalm, and in singing the hymn, so appropriate to their feelings—

" God moves in a mysterious way,
His wonders to perform."

Most truly did their thankful hearts express themselves in these words. After this, the three little ones went away together, running first to tell everything to Minny, to whom Ida was nearly as much attached as were the other children.

"Blessins on you, Miss Ida," said Minny ; " I'se dredful glad ob all de happy tings dat's come to pass, by de good Lord shining His glory on dis family. De Lord brings you to dis place, where de old man learns to love de Saviour, and den · you is taken right up by dese good people, and de Lord brings your father and mother right ober to dis land, jes as soon as His right hand has ebery ting ready, and den He puts you right, sure nuff, in your father's arms. Blessed be de name of de good Lord." And Minny's bright turban shook with her earnestness.

"We thanked Him to-night, dear Minny," said Ida.

"Blessins on you," said Minny; "we can never tank and praise Him nuff."

"Minny, sing about it," said Mary, "and we will do the chorus."

Minny's turban began to nod, and in a few moments her clear voice rang out her praises, in the following words:

> Tanks to de Lord, and gib Him praise,
> Now, chil'n, high your voices raise,
>   In singing Hallelujah.
> Praise first our Saviour crucified,
> Praise Him, who came to earth and died,
>   Praise Him in Hallelujah.
>
> Praise Him who rose in glory too,
> Praise Him! 'tis little we can do,
>   But praise in Hallelujah!
> Praise Him, de life, de trouf, de way,
> Praise Him, who guards us ebery day,
>   Praise Him in Hallelujah!

He saw de little lamb dat strayed,
He heard her parents when dey prayed.
    Praise Him in Hallelujah.
De lamb was guarded by His arm,
No thorns nor briers did it harm,
    Praise Him in Hallelujah !

It felt de sunshine ob His love,
It learned for help to look above,
    And praise in Hallelujah !
And den He showed His loving hand,
And brought de parents to dis land,
    To praise in Hallelujah !

For here de little lamb was seen,
Feeding in pastures still and green,
    And singing Hallelujah !
So let us eber love and praise,
And daily den, our voices raise
    And shout our Hallelujah !"

As soon as Minny's clear ringing voice was heard, Mr. Montgomerie opened the library door, and motioned to Mr. Dorris to come to the foot of the stairs. Not a word was lost, but Mr. Dorris was utterly bewildered at the strange words, the way in which they were sung, and the outburst of Hallelujahs from the children.

19

"What does it mean?" he asked, as they returned to the library.

Mr. Montgomerie said: "I could not help giving your English ears a specimen of one of our pious southern negroes. Our nurse was set free by her master, who was a friend of my mother's, and Minny was sent to us. She is a real character, truly and simply a Christian, and with a heart so full of thanksgiving, that every event of life is to her a song of praise. She begins to sing. The words, in some simple rhyming measure, seem to pour out of her heart, and the children join in the chorus, which always characterizes the southern melodies. It is as natural to them to say ' Minny, sing it,' as it is easy to her to give her thoughts this expression. She sways her body backwards and forwards, her eyes shine, her turban nods, and in fact she reminds me of an ancient pythoness. I'll introduce you to her to-morrow."

"I don't know that I can bear many more surprises," he returned; " my brain fairly reels

under its load of joy; and I also long to relieve my poor wife's anxiety. Will you read
the document of which you told me, for I
want to know everything that you can tell of
my child."

Mr. Montgomerie briefly explained how
they came to be interested in Mariano, read
grandma's note, described their going to hear
his account of himself and the child, and then
said :

"I must have your promise, that if accident
should reveal the persons who really stole
your child, you will not prosecute them, for
Mariano's sake ?"

Mr. Dorris looked thoughtful for a moment,
then said : "I promise." Mr. Montgomerie
then read the paper. It seemed of deeper
interest than ever, and old 'Mariano and
Mariti found a place in the heart of Mr. Dorris.

The funeral was described. Grandma told
all she could of Ida, whom she had learned
not only to love but to respect. She is un-
demonstrative," she said, "but has deep feel-

ings ; she is thoroughly truthful, and desirous of doing exactly right, at any cost to herself. Her manner is refined ; there has no coarseness come to her during her wandering life ; she has every element with which to form a noble woman. Her devotion to Mariano, her sensitiveness lest any blame should attach to him, makes her even more careful to prove, by her own behavior, how faithful he was to her. Her knowledge of religion is only recent. I have taught her but little besides our Lord's ministry of love, and that she has received gladly. The Bible is a new book to her. In general knowledge she is, of course, deficient. She reads and speaks well, and has a wonderful memory. So, my dear Mr. Dorris, you have a fine foundation on which to rear a grand super-structure. Her loss to me will be great, and after you and Mrs. Dorris have learned to realize your blessing, I want you all to return here and pass the spring and summer with me."

" Thank you, thank you. All such plans I

must leave until Mrs. Dorris and I can decide what will be best. I propose, with your permission, dear madam, to take my child to her mother to-morrow, by the mid-day train. We must have our treasure together as soon as possible."

"That is but natural," said Mr. Montgomerie ; "but let me suggest that you return here, and pass the Easter holidays, after which you can make mother a visit as long as she can persuade you to stay. We would rather have you here, but I feel that mother really has the stronger claim."

"I think this will be very delightful, and I will consult Mrs. Dorris. By the by, what became of that monkey ?"

This unexpected question was answered by a general laugh. "Thank you for asking," said Mr. Montgomerie ; "that monkey has been a great cause of embarrassment to us. Ida expends an amount of love and care on it that may trouble or please you. It depends on how you take it."

"Do not fear. I could accept a menagerie with Ida, and I shall take it with great philosophy, but where is it?"

Mrs. Montgomerie said, in explanation: "Ida's natural delicacy seemed to see that you might not wish to be required to receive her and her pet at the same time, so she left it with one of my servants until to-morrow, or longer, if you wish. I think you had better take Ida first, and let Mrs. Dorris be introduced to Jocko, as you were, through Mariano's story, after which, I will send John down to the city with him, unless he continues to be contented, in which case he can remain."

"Thank you, that is an admirable plan, and as I do not know how Mrs. Dorris will like it at first, I will accept your offer. I must own that my daughter with a monkey on her shoulder would have startled me a little. Her mother will be a little prepared through the thoughtfulness of Mrs. Montgomerie in sending, to-night, a copy of Mariano's account."

At this moment, William announced supper, which mamma had ordered, because she had noticed that Mr. Dorris could not succeed in eating any dinner.

"Thank you," said he, offering her his arm. "I was just beginning to feel that human nature must have some sustenance besides joy."

Soon after supper, they separated for the night, but it was a long time before sleep visited any member of the happy household.

XX.

Good-bye, Ida.

THE next morning, it was late before the family gathered around the breakfast-table, and soon after, Mr. Dorris and Ida bade farewell to Brightside and its hospitable inmates, to drive with grandma to Burnside, where Ida could prepare what was needed to go to the city, and from there to the depot, for the train which would reach New York at four o'clock.

The hope of being soon re-united prevented the parting from being a sad one, and as the day was warm for the season, the drive was very pleasant. Ida was greeted at Burnside with such a storm of joy, by Polly, Jocko and Jip, that Mr. Dorris whispered to grandma :

" I am glad I said I would accept a menagerie
with Ida. Are these all her pets ?"

" No, indeed," said grandma. " I can only
spare her one of them, and I shall regret to
part with Jocko."

Ida was delighted with her father's reception of her wonderful monkey, who behaved
very well ; did whatever he was told, with
great sagacity, and then mounted the cornice,
and relieved his mind by making faces at Mr.
Dorris.

There was not much time for anything but
preparations and lunch, after which, Mr.
Dorris looked at his watch and said : " Now,
Ida, we must go."

Ida hesitated a moment, then said : " Grandma, may I speak to you a moment, if papa
will excuse me ?"

They went into another room.

" Grandma, dear, I cannot thank you, you
know I love you. If father and mother had
not come, I would have been your little girl.
We are coming back soon, and, perhaps, will

be here this summer ; and grandma, will you please tell Nora about my going so suddenly, and thank her for what she said to me. Please tell her I have found a great many reasons now to love my Saviour."

"My darling child !" exclaimed grandma, "what shall I do without you ? You are very, very dear to me. May our Father ever have you in His holy keeping. Good-bye, my dear little girl."

Mr. Montgomerie met Mr. Dorris at the depot ; and Ida looked her farewell from the window, as long as she could see him.

Grandma found it hard to do without the bright little girl, who fed the birds, and who clung so closely to her all day ; but she began, at once, some active duty, which occupied her, though she rather dreaded the quiet dinner. Just before it was served, a carriage drove up, and Henry and Mary jumped out, with faithful Minny.

"Oh, grandma, dear, we thought you would be lonely, and we persuaded mamma to let us

come over to dinner. Ar'n't you very glad to
see us ?" said Mary, the chief speaker.

"I'm *very* glad. I can't tell you how glad,
for I was just thinking how lonely my dinner
would be."

"Now I said so," said Mary. "I knew you
would miss Ida. Oh, Henry, there's Jocko,
isn't it lovely to have him ?"

Jocko and Polly and Jip had so much to
say about it, acccording to the different ways
in which nature permitted them to express
themselves, that dinner had to be delayed
until affairs were "deranged," as Mary said.

When they went into dinner, a very awk-
ward thing happened. Jocko insisted upon
sitting on John's shoulder. How he could wait
upon the table with this addition he did not
seem to see. Henry and Mary, and even
grandma, could not help laughing, and tried
to take Jocko, but, no ! he would stay there
and nowhere else. John tried to go through
the usual routine, but his dignity suffered
greatly, for the children could hardly eat for

laughing, and Jocko chattered so at them, and directly in John's ear, that at last he rushed out of the room, and his efforts to suppress his merriment, until he reached the kitchen, were irresistible to the others.

Presently Minny appeared: "Please, Mis' Gomerie, let me try and wait on de table. Dat monkey cre'tur has took hold on John so dat he can't do nothing."

Anything unusual delighted the children, and Minny did her best to fill John's place— her turban appearing and disappearing with the dishes, as grandma said, like a "peripatetic bouquet."

"Oh, what *does* that mean? A petatic bouquet. It's a delightful new word. Do tell me, grandma?" begged Mary.

Grandma had only said it to hear Mary try, so she replied: "A bouquet that walks about, try again, peripatetic."

"Oh dear, dear, peri-pa-ta-tet-tic"—

"No. Now, Harry, you try."

Henry was more successful, and after awhile

Mary learned it well enough, she thought, to say it as soon as she had an opportunity.

They had a great deal to talk of; for Ida's wonderful story was an unfailing source of interest, and whether she would come back, and how she would like her mamma and New York, and so on, were all discussed.

"It seems strange to ask how she would like her mamma," said Henry; "as if anybody could do anything else!"

"I don't know about that," said Mary. "I think some mammas in story books are not one bit nice."

"Perhaps," explained grandma, "because the story books tell about some particular thing that the mother does, which you may not like, but does not tell all the loving things, and good things, which she does. You know a book cannot tell everything."

"Yes, grandma," said Henry, "maybe the mammas in books put their children to bed, and kiss them and all."

"Ellen Montgomerie's mother was lovely,

but Daisy Randolph's was dreadful," said Mary, referring to her two favorite books (" The Wide, Wide World," and " Melbourne House); " but, grandma, can't we hurry with dinner, and have a good play before papa comes for us ?"

The 'good play' was much enjoyed, and Polly and Jip were as merry as the rest, but Jocko would not leave John, who was obliged to do all his work with him on his shoulder, or swinging by one paw to his collar, and chattering all the time. It amused the children very much. When the time nearly came for them to go, Mary said :

"Now, grandma dear, you're not to be miserable about Ida. We will do all we can to comfort you, and when you feel dull you must come over to Brightside, and we will 'Shine you up,' as Minny says. I wish we could live in both places, don't you, Harry ?"

"Yes ; and I think we do. I feel as if we belong here."

" You do, dear children, and I thank you

for this little happy visit. I miss Ida very much, for I thought she might live with me. You know it is lonely sometimes since my little boy went away."

"Why, grandma, who was your 'little boy.' Do you mean papa?"

"Yes, dear, he was my little boy once, then he grew to be a big boy, and went to live at Brightside. I think it is all right, but sometimes I am a little bit lonely, but"—said grandma, looking bright again, "then you come, or some one to cheer me, or I have something to do; but there is my little boy now."

"Come in, grandma's little boy," said Mary. Papa laughed, and Polly began:

"Come in, come in, Home, sweet Home."

Papa sat down to talk a little while, during which time, the children were trying to induce Jocko to come to them, but he would not leave John. So at last they gave it up, and bade him good-bye.

In a few days after, Mr. Dorris and Ida left. Very grateful letters were received from Mrs.

Dorris, full of her new found treasure, whom she seemed to think perfectly lovely, and perfectly beautiful, and that there never were parents more blessed. The agony of the past years, she said, was forgotten, and life seemed all joy. At the close of the letter to Mrs. Montgomerie, she said :

"Now, my dear old friend, Louise, I want you all to come to us, and share our happiness. We have left the noisy St. Nicholas, and are in delightful rooms at the Fifth Avenue. We are entirely private, and can give you a fine suite of six rooms adjoining ours. I want to see the wonderful Minny also, and I hope you will not disappoint us. Then we will pass the Easter holidays with you, and make a short visit to Ida's 'grandma' at Burnside. After which we will travel in this country for a few months, and then we hope once more to have a home at Dorris Park. It seems too far in the future for plans. But we expect, as soon as we can restore it to its former condition, that you will come to us there.

It is more than six years since we have lived
there, for we had been absent a year, when
Ida was taken from us—our beautiful golden-
haired darling !—and we have never returned.
She brought me the curl saved by that dear
old man.   How I wish I could thank him.
But I will leave all else till we meet.

"I forgot the monkey ! We have sent for
him.   I must acknowledge to a preference
for Ida without her pet.   But I shall keep
this unworthy sentiment a secret, and en-
deavor to accept him with composure.   I
certainly would prefer to introduce my
daughter without this evidence of her past
life ; but, at present, I see no way to escape
this permanent addition to our family.   If you
can suggest a remedy, pray add to the num-
berless reasons for which, I sign myself, ever
gratefully and lovingly yours,

"LETA DORRIS."

"Very delightfully planned by our charming friend ; but, Lulu, not at all the best thing

for our little ones. Shall we go, dear?" asked Mr. Montgomerie.

"I think we had better go for a few days. I must see my old friend, Leta, as soon as possible. If mother goes, we will trust Minny with the children. If not they can go to Burnside, for we could not take them to the city at this season of furnaces and childrens' maladies, even if we were willing to take them to a hotel," replied Mrs. Montgomerie.

"Shall we tell them, or will it be too great a disappointment?"

"I think we had better keep to our rule of telling them whatever concerns them or ourselves. We cannot shield them from the usual disappointments of life."

"I agree with you, dear, but I want to ask, why you did not tell Mary the reason that she was not permitted to come to our dinner-party. In fact, I felt a little curiosity myself."

"Did I not tell you? I certainly had no wish to keep it from you, although I thought it would make the matter of too much importance if I told Mary. Sometime ago, at one of our dinners, Mrs. Folly exclaimed, as Mary entered, 'What a lovely picture ! my child, you are too· beautiful to be real !' Mary looked rather astonished, but I found she lingered beside Mrs. Folly for the rest of the evening, evidently pleased with the flattery.

"I never have concealed from the children that they have the gift of attractive looks, but I have taught them to consider this as one of the lesser gifts, and one that is really controlled by the character, the loveliest face being deformed by a fretful disposition. That was all. You see why it was better Mary should not know. Suppose we go over and dine with mother to-day, then we can know what she will do, and reply to Leta at once."

This was done. Grandma could not possibly leave her schools and sick people in the winter, when nearly every one else had left their country homes, so that Henry and Mary were to stay at Burnside during their papa's and mamma's absence.

XXI.

About Old Friends and Dear Friends.

NOW, as grandma told Mary, "story books cannot tell everything," so this story book cannot tell what a delightful visit Henry and Mary made at Burnside, or what an equally delightful one their papa and mamma had in New York, nor how rapidly the little dogs grew, nor how Henry and Mary studied all they could in the gospels about the rising of Christ. The reason is, that the book would be too large, and you might be tired of reading so many pages: so we will leave out everything that happened at Brightside and Burnside, say no more about what Nora, or Ida, or Miss Sables did during that time, and begin again on the Saturday when Mr. and Mrs. Dorris, Ida, the monkey, the man-servant, and the maid-servant, ten trunks, two dressing-cases, four umbrellas and two canes, ·a gun case, a lunch basket, and two large rolls of shawls and travelling blankets in straps, arrived at Brightside at three o'clock.

Ida was seized by Henry and Mary, and carried first to Minny, then to see all the rooms that were ready for her father and mother, while Mr. and Mrs. Dorris were having a hearty welcome down-stairs. As soon as the luggage was disposed of, they went to their rooms to rest and refresh themselves before dinner. Ida promised to come back to the children, as soon as her mamma could spare her, which she very kindly did, after tea had been sent up to the rooms.

There was so much to show Ida before dinner, that she was hurried at once to the stable, where the dogs had improved so greatly; she honestly confessed that she could not have taught them better herself. "But where's Dash?" she asked.

"Oh dear!" exclaimed Mary, "that was another 'strastrophy. One night, they all climbed over the board at the door, and fell down the stairs, at least the little ones did (I don't believe Carlo did), and got among the horses, and I suppose one of them stepped on Dash, for he was dead, and darling Carlo's right hand back leg was hurt. He must have gone to see about Dash. Wasn't it dreadful?"

"Indeed it was. I'm *so* sorry. What did Carlo say in the morning?"

"Tom found them," said Henry, "he says, all together by the door, and all crying. Poor little doggies. I hope they have forgotten now."

"When is Carlo coming to live with you?" asked Ida.

"Not till warm weather. Tom is going to keep Dandy himself, and to give Fido away, and we will take Carlo. We want him very much, but it seems so hard to separate the family."

"Yes, that *is* hard. Now let us go to Frolic, I have lots of sugar for him."

Frolic was delighted to see them, and enjoyed the sugar very much.

"How do you read his blanket?" asked Ida. "Is it Henry Frolic, or Frolic Henry?"

"I think it is Frolic's Henry," said Mary; "for Henry does more for Frolic than he does for Henry." Frolic whinnied again. "There, he says 'yes,' you see."

"Now we have something new," said Henry; "papa brought it to us from New York. Tom please bring out the *new* pony-phaeton."

In a few minutes a beautiful little carriage, in which a well-trained goat was harnessed, was brought out. It would only hold two, and Mary said: "Jump in, Ida, Henry will drive you round the place. Take this blanket. Isn't it soft and lovely? Mamma brought us this, but it is almost too warm to-day to need it. I will run home now."

Ida and Henry drove off, delighted with the little "turnout," as Tom called it. After a few minutes of admiration, Henry asked Ida how she liked everything in New York.

. "Why, Harry," said Ida, "I suppose I am perfectly happy. Papa and mamma are kind and loving. I believe they would give me the moon if they could, but, Harry, don't tell anybody, for I am afraid it's my wicked heart. Sometimes I feel as if I couldn't live another minute without seeing grandfather, and as the spring comes on, I know I shall want to go travelling off in the country, with him and Jocko."

"But, Ida dear, you are going travelling all over, everywhere."

"Yes, I know, shut up in cars, but I want to wander about. Oh, Harry, we used to sit down under the trees, and grandfather would tell me about Mariti, and describe the birds and flowers of Italy, and the blue waters of the sea, and the fishing, and he and I meant to go back there and live, and I was to take care of his house for him. Then sometimes he would say, 'But, maybe, I'm too old. If I am Mariti will do what is best for us.' He was so like a child, it wasn't like being with a grown-up man."

"But, dear Ida, he died you know, so you never could have gone back. Why don't you ask your papa and mamma to take you out there, to see the old place where he lived?"

"Oh, Harry, that is a lovely idea. I will ask them. I know they will, and I never thought of it. I am going to the grave to-morrow. Dear mamma bought me some flowers, called immortelles, which will not fade. She says in Italy and France the people put them on graves, and so that's what grandfather would have had on his if he had been buried beside Mariti, at Cetara."

"That's nice, isn't it?" replied Henry.

"Yes, indeed. I kissed her a hundred times for that, but I *do* want to see grandfather, so!"

"Ida," said Henry, gravely, "I'm afraid it *is* your heart. I don't mean to say so in a hard way, and I don't think it's wrong in you to think about your grandfather, but it seems to me as if you don't let yourself be happy."

"Harry, I will try, and—I have made up my mind to give Jocko away."

"Oh, how can you?" he exclaimed.

"Why, Harry, I know he worries mamma, and he is a great deal of trouble. He is so full of mischief that I can hardly leave him a minute. It was so different when I had very little to do but take care of him, or when we lived in plain rooms, or were walking round the country. Now he sees so many strange things he is half crazy. He stops the clocks, tears the lace curtains, examines mamma's dressing-case, pours out the cologne, and, oh, I can't tell you all he does. Then, Harry, when we go to drive in a fine carriage, all dressed up, I know a monkey is not the right kind of a pet to have."

"That will be very hard, dear Ida, but I see that it would be better. Whom will you give him to?"

"I have thought about Nora, but I must find out how she is, and whether she wants him."

"We must go home now, Ida, there is Mary on the piazza. Have you had a nice drive? I couldn't help the roads being muddy, you know. The frost is still coming out."

"Oh, I've had a lovely time. I like the mud, it's so soft after those rattling streets. Don't tell about my feelings."

Henry promised, as he drew up Browser (the goat) at the steps. Mary helped Ida out, Tom took the carriage, and the children ran to welcome grandma, who had just come.

Ida's joy at seeing her earliest friend again, was more quiet than the daily reception she had from Mary, but too deep and earnest to doubt its truth.

Indeed, grandma never doubted anything. If any one said they loved her, she believed it; if a servant said she tried to do right, she believed it ; and her faith in goodness really seemed to make people do better. They were ashamed to do wrong when Mrs. Montgomerie was so sure they did not mean to. She was so active and energetic that she did not think any one could be indolent. She was always sure they were ill, if they were what is called lazy, and generally proposed cold water bathing or tonics, and sympathized so kindly in their sufferings, that many a person who much preferred lying on a sofa and reading, was induced to get up, simply to prove that she could do so. But I must go on with the story. The dinner at six o'clock was a very joyful one. Mrs. Dorris had recovered her health and beauty, and her eyes darted such beams of light at Ida, that they were wonderful to see.

The children were so important a part of both families that they were permitted to talk, although some of the conversation was rather beyond their comprehension, for the elders of the party were full of natural wit and brilliancy, besides the highest culture. Mary heard a great many new words, which she tried hard to remember, and once when somebody spoke to her, started so suddenly, that

mamma said : " Where are your thoughts,
my daughter ?"

" Excuse me, mamma, I was studying gip
tollery."

It was too much to resist. A merry ring
of laughter followed her speech, and Mary's
fancy for new words had to be explained.
Mr. Dorris comforted her, by saying : " Come
to me, after dinner, Miss Mary, and I'll tell
you all about it, and about anything else you
want to know."

The evening was a very happy one, for
besides the pleasure of all being together, a
very large box stood in the hall, directed to
Henry and Mary. William soon opened it,
and a megaletescope was taken out, which Mr.
and Mrs. Dorris had brought to the children.
They were delighted with it, and a half-hour
had to be added to eight o'clock that it could
be examined. Mary tried hard to say the
name, but meggelscope was as near as she
could come to it. At last they were obliged
to say " Good-night," and grandma made Ida's

heart very grateful by saying, "I must see Jocko before I go. Is he as comical as ever?"

"Not quite, dear grandma, he is so often in disgrace. He does not understand that if he could run up a tree and pull off the apples, he may not run up a curtain and pull off the ornaments of the cornice. Mamma is very patient with him, but I ought to give him away, and not let him annoy her."

"My poor darling, I was afraid he would not do for city life. How would you like to trust him with Nora? She is able to walk now, and would be delighted to have him and the organ too."

"I had thought of Nora, and am glad you think it a good plan, here he is." Jocko's face brightened up at seeing his little mistress again, and showed his love by various monkey tricks. He certainly was as pretty a creature as a monkey could be; his beautiful mouse-colored fur was soft and clean, and grandma was sorry to part him from Ida, but she told her she would come on Monday and take her to Nora if she wished. Ida was really anxious to relieve her mamma, and promised to go, for, as she said : " If he is very unhappy, then I will have time to find some other home for him."

Henry and Mary called grandma to come and kiss them good-night, for, said they, " We are going to sleep right off, to be ready for Sunday."

Soon after this, grandma returned home, having a promise of a visit from Mr. and Mrs. Dorris, after they had passed a week at Brightside. A few hours of conversation finished the evening.

XXII.

Easter-Sunday.

THE sun seemed to shine more brightly than ever, in the east window of the nursery, as Minny opened the door on the Resurrection morning. Her heart warmed in its light and glory, as she stood directly in its golden sheen.

Minny, in her simple faith and heart of love, had no memory of the sun-worship of her ancestors, but the wonder of the light and warmth made their source to her an emblem of that glory that no man can approach unto. She once explained her feelings about it to Mrs. Montgomerie in the following words :

" It's de *nearest* we can come to knowing what de glory ob de light can be, and though de sunshine is only one ob de lights dat de

Lord made, it's de one near to us, and de one de Lord made for us, and when I read 'bout de Sun ob Righteousness rising wid healing in His wings, I know de Lord meant to 'splain it to us by letting de warm sun rise in de blue sky, and spread its glory ober de mountains and de valleys, and to go into de windows, and to shine into de homes of de people, and onto de sick people; making dem feel well and 'trong. It's *one* ob de pictures de good Lord put in His book for His people to larn by."

And Minny learnt by this one of the Lord's pictures, and taught those she loved the same beautiful lesson.

As she stood gazing on the clear light, looking on it make "de world glorysome," watching the shining evergreens, the early blue birds, her thoughts went back to that garden where the flowers bloomed around the Lord's sepulchre, and her eyes brightened with the imagination of the light which shone upon them as He, the King of Glory, burst the

21

bondage of the tomb. At this moment Henry opened his door with the words,

"Minny! The Lord hath risen!"

"He hath risen, indeed!" returned Minny, prepared for the Easter-morning greeting of the early Christians, and, in an instant, her thoughts found expression in song:

> Give Him praise and honor den,
>   He is de King ob Glory!
> He came, He lived, He died for men,
>   Jesus! de King ob Glory.
> He conquered death, He lives again,
>   A living King ob Glory,
> O'er heaven and earth He'll eber reign,
>   Eternal King ob Glory!

"Oh, Minny," said Henry, "I don't believe there's anybody like you in the world. You always sing out my thoughts. I don't see how you do it."

"*I* don't do it no how, Mas'r Harry. I jes opens my heart and de words come right out, and dere's tunes to all de words, it's de way tings is made I 'spect, only I opens my heart, oder people keeps deirs shut. Now go on wid

getting dressed. De breakfast will soon be
ready, and I'll leave out all de tings, 'cause I
want to shine up little Nora on de way to de
Lord's House. De missis has a picture for her,
wid flowers growing ober a cross, see dere!
I'm to take it to her."

"Oh, isn't that lovely? And, Minny, do
you know the surprise that's ready for Ida?"

"No, I neber heard noting."

"Why, Minny, Ida's father and mother
have had a beautiful plain polished granite
cross put over Mariano's grave. And, after
church, we are to take Ida there in the carriage. Ida brought up from New York some
everlasting flowers for a wreath, to leave on
the grave, and she will be so surprised to see
the cross. Mamma will give her some green-
house flowers too, but they wont last, you
know. And Ida says these she has, will stay
alive for years and years. We are all to go
together to the Sunday-school this afternoon.
And the chapel children from the mission are
coming over. They have the lesson that we

have been learning about the Resurrection, and Mr. Watkins is to hear us. I'm so glad it's a nice warm day!"

"Yes, de good Lord makes dis day most glorysome. I must go, Mas'r Harry, de missis will 'tend to de little service dis morning."

After breakfast, the carriages came to take them all to church. Mr. and Mrs. Dorris, and Mr. and Mrs. Montgomerie in the large carriage, the three children in the smaller one. They met at the door of the church, and little Ida, so well known as the organ-grinder's child, walked up the aisle with her parents, all unconscious of the interest she excited.

Of all the services of the Episcopal Church, those appointed in memory of the Resurrection are the most full of holy joy. The suggestions of the day, the opening spring, all add to the interest of the services which are so appropriately beautiful. Henry and Mary never were permitted to go to church ignorant of the meaning of the chapters which they would there hear read, or of the reason why they were chosen for that time ; so that they were prepared not only to unite in the psalms and hymns, but to understand the twelfth chapter of Exodus, which tells of the Passover, and how the sprinkling of the blood of the lamb on the doorposts saved the lives of the firstborn of Israel, and how it taught the redemption through the blood of Christ. Also in the sixth of Romans—which is the second lesson for the day,—how eternal life is the gift of God. And in the epistle for the day they knew that St. Paul, was telling the Colossians, how they ought to love Jesus Christ, who had risen from the dead, and would appear again in glory. That the gospel told about the disciples going to the sepulchre, and of what they discovered there. So these little children listened intelligently.

It was a good deal of trouble to teach all this to their children, but Mr. and Mrs. Montgomerie counted it one of their duties, and made it a part of their life-work ; and Henry and Mary were so anxious to learn, so ready to be taught, that the duty was a pleasure.

They were quiet and attentive to the service and tried to understand the sermon, but it was, as Mary might have said, very figurative. So they only had a general impression that Christ's rising from the tomb rolled something away from the hearts of people.

In this they were right.

When the services for the day were concluded, Henry, Mary and Ida went quietly out of church to the carriage, which was waiting for them at the door, and Tom drove them to the gate of the little cemetery. Ida had her basket of rare green-house flowers, with the wreath of immortelles, and, talking of how they would arrange them, they left the carriage and walked on to the grave. It was a warm and bright day for the season. The blue birds and robins were singing their welcome to the Spring. The grass was beginning to look green, where it was not shaded from the sun. Crocusses and daffodils were lifting up their little heads to tell their story of the Easter.

"How lovely everything is," said Ida. "I am so glad we came to-day, but oh! what is that? Oh, who has put that lovely cross there?"

They had just come in sight of the grave, and the pure granite cross was seen at its head. There was nothing on the cross, but on a slab of granite, at the foot of the grave, and supported on low pillars, was the following inscription, read first to herself, and then aloud to her companions:

"IN PACE!     FIDELIS.

In grateful memory
of
The faithful guardian
of their child,
This monument is erected
by
Albert and Leta Dorris,
to
Mariano Zachiti,
A native of Amalfi, Italy,
who died in this town,
aged, nearly 80 years.

'I will give unto this last, even
as unto thee.' "

Ida said nothing, she could not speak.
Henry handed her the wreath, she hung it on
the cross, and then lovingly and reverentially
laid the flowers at its foot.   They stood still
a moment, then Ida spoke : " From this moment I devote myself to my precious father
and mother.   Oh, how good and kind they
are !"

" Dear Ida," said Henry, " I'm so glad for
you."

" And," said Mary, " when you have gone
far away, maybe mamma will let us put some
flowers here for you.   How beautiful those
bright flowers look at the foot of the cross."

" Everything is lovely," said Ida, as they
turned away.   " I did not know I could be so
happy."

The effect of this kind thoughtfulness on
the part of Ida's parents, was to prove to Ida
that she had been mistaken in thinking that
her past life was painful to them.   They had

carved their gratitude to Mariano in stone, that every one might read, and surely they could not have been ashamed of him. This was all that had prevented her from giving them all her love, so that her face, though serious, was now happier in its expression than her loving father or mother had ever before seen it. She went at once to them, on their return from church, and simply, but gracefully, expressed her gratitude. There was not much time to talk, for lunch was ready, and at three o'clock they were all to be at the chapel, for the Sunday-school exercises.

Mary found time to ask Henry what all the top part of the writing on the stone meant. "The foreign language I mean, Harry," she said.

"That's Latin and Greek," said Henry; "papa told me all about it. It's a copy of something that is on one of the tombs of the early Christians."

"What are they? Do you mean get-up-early-in-the-morning Christians, like grandma?" asked Mary.

"No, no ; you funny child. I mean those people who were Christians in the beginning of the Christian religion. A great many of them lived at Rome, and some of them were killed for being Christians. Then their friends took their bodies to a place under ground, and buried them in secret. And what is on Mariano's stone was copied from one of the tombs in that underground place."

"How 'straordinary!" said Mary. "Now, what does it mean?"

"In pace, means, in peace ; and fidelis, means, faithful. That suited Mariano, you know, for everybody says he was a faithful old man."

"Yes," said Mary, "did all he knew, I suppose. Now what about P and X.

"That isn't P and X, it's two Greek letters, pronounced Rho and Chi."

"Dear! I wonder if I'll ever know so much! Tell me quick what they mean before I forget their names."

"Papa told me all about it, before we went

to the grave. You must say Chi, first, because that stands for Ch, then Rho, because that stands for R, and Chr are the three first letters of the name of Christ, and those letters put together that way, make a monogram."

" What is that hard word, Harry ?"

" That means that several letters are written together in one, like what mamma has on her note paper, only this one is made of Greek letters, Chi Rho, printed together."

" Thank you, Henry, it's a dreadful long story. What's the name of those underground places ?"

" You keep asking me questions," replied Henry, laughing, " and I can't help the answers being long. The name of those places is catacombs."

" Can't listen any more, I shall forget all my Easter lesson for this afternoon. Come, lunch is ready. How we do have to hurry on Easters and such days !"

At lunch, there was some conversation

upon the sermon of the morning. The children were called upon to repeat the text. Ida instantly did so. "And they found the stone rolled away from the sepulchre," she said.

"It was an excellent sermon," said Mr. Dorris; "so full of hope, and one that our new-found joy renders it easier for us to feel. A month ago, I seemed to have a stone on my heart that could never be removed."

"It is hard for us to feel that the same loving Lord is with us in sorrow as in joy, and the words, 'Rejoice evermore. In everything give thanks,' seem as if they were not meant for us when our hearts are pressed down with grief," said Mr. Montgomerie.

"The gospel was *good* tidings of *great joy*," said Mrs. Montgomerie; "and mother impresses that upon all whom she can influence."

"But," said Mrs. Dorris, "how we forget all that in the selfishness of sorrow."

"And we forget, too, that there is no precept or command given that it is impossible to keep. Even our prayers and supplications must be offered with *thanksgiving*," said Mr. Dorris. "But did you say we must be at the chapel at three o'clock? It is past two now."

They were soon ready. They drove to the chapel, but were to walk home.

The children took their seats in Miss Sables' class, and much enjoyed the entrance of the Mission-school, and the preparatory exercises and hymns.

I must begin another chapter to tell you about the lesson, because I want you to understand it, and to want to read all about it in the four gospels.

XXIII.

The Lesson at the Sunday-school.

"NOW, dear children," said Mr. Watkins, "I am very happy to see so many of you in your places, for this is one of the joyful days of the Church year. The rising of our Lord is what we celebrate to-day, and we make it a joyful feast. We do this because His Resurrection was a reason for the whole world to be happy. It was one of the many proofs that He was truly God, and it was also both a prophecy and a promise to us, that like as Christ rose from the dead so shall we rise and live again. St. Paul tries to explain this to the church at Corinth, by telling about grain which is sown in the ground; 'bare grain' he calls it; which dies, he says, and then is 'quickened,' or comes to life, and grows up, pushing its way through the ground, until it rises in whatever beautiful form God chooses to give it. You can try it yourselves: you can plant a grain of wheat: it will come up a little green stem ; then a flowery head will appear ; and then grains of wheat will be formed, in this head. Just as our Saviour said, 'first the blade, then the ear, after that the full corn in the ear.' St. Paul meant to explain that our bodies must be put in the ground after we die and turn to dust, until the time of the resurrection or rising, and then, like as Christ rose, even so shall we rise. Now, dear children, we bring flowers around us on Easter day because they help us to understand this subject. Look at this callah, see how white, and pure and beautiful it is, and yet it was put in the ground a dark colored little seed. It turned to dust ; the life in the seed grew and burst through the ground ; a little stem and leaves came up, and at last God gave it this beautiful form. As St. Paul says, 'A body as it hath pleased Him, to every seed its own body,' and each one distinct and different according to the seed that is put in.

"Now this cannot exactly explain this wonderful subject to us, because the life of plants is not *exactly* like our life, and the vegetable life that enables them to grow up out of the earth is not *exactly* like the spiritual life that will be in us when we live again, and neither was the rising of Christ *exactly* like what ours will be. His body did not turn to dust. The Bible says He could not see corruption, which means, His body could not decay, but ours must do so. After the spirit had left our Saviour's body, His lifeless form was on Friday afternoon laid in the tomb, and on the Jewish Sabbath, our Saturday, it was still there, but on the next day, our Sunday, His spirit entered into it again, and our Lord rose from the tomb, because, as St. Peter said, it was not possible that He could be 'holden by death.'

"Now, you may not understand all that I have told you, but this you know (and if you

learn one such truth each day it will be enough),
you know that Christ Jesus, the Lord of Glory,
rose from His tomb or sepulchre, a living man.
Where was this sepulchre, dear children, was
it in a dreary, lonely place ?"

" No, sir. It was in a garden, near to the
place where Jesus was crucified."

" Whose tomb was it ? Did it belong to one
of the twelve disciples ?"

" No, sir, it belonged to Joseph of Arima-
thea."

" What is said about him ?"

" He was a rich man. He was a counsellor,
a good man and a just."

" Had he approved of the crucifixion ?"

" No, indeed, he had not consented to the
counsel and deed of them," said one of the boys.

" What is meant by the rest of that verse,
' who also himself waited for the kingdom of
God ' ?"

" It means," said one of the girls, " that he
was, like Simeon, waiting for the ' consolation
of Israel.' "

" Who was the consolation of Israel ?" asked Mr. Watkins, of the one who answered last.

" Jesus Christ. He was ' the light to lighten the Gentiles, and the glory of Israel.' "

" Yes, indeed He was ; and we are the Gentiles, and He is our light, and He is the King, and His kingdom, Joseph the counsellor waited for. Now tell me more about Joseph. Had he been a brave, outspoken Christian, or had he feared to say that he loved Jesus of Nazareth ?"

" He used to be afraid ; he was a disciple ' secretly for fear of the Jews ;' but when Jesus died, I suppose he was sorry, for St. Mark says ' he went boldly unto Pilate, and craved the body of Jesus.' "

" Do you think any other disciple was sorry for the same thing."

" I think Nicodemus must have been, for he brought spices, and helped Joseph, and, together, they ' wound the body in linen clothes, with the spices.' Oh ! they must have been very sorry !"

" Yes, dear children, very sorry, I am sure, as every one will be, who fears to say before the world, ' I am a Christian.' Before we continue the questions, let us sing :

> " Jesus, and shall it ever be,
> A mortal man ashamed of Thee ;
> Ashamed of Thee, whom angels praise,
> Whose glories shine through endless days.
>
> " Ashamed of Jesus ! sooner far
> Let night disown each radiant star ;
> 'Tis midnight with my soul, till He,
> Bright Morning Star, bid darkness flee.
>
> " Ashamed of Jesus ! empty pride,
> I'll boast a Saviour crucified:
> And, O may this my portion be,
> My Saviour's not ashamed of me."

" How did Joseph and Nicodemus show their love, now that they were no longer afraid ?"

" I think they took the best spices and ointment they could buy, and linen, which is called ' fine linen.' "

" Yes, dear children, I am sure it was the best they could give Him then, and after they had tenderly prepared the body for the tomb, they carried it among the lovely flowers that were blooming in that Eastern garden, and laid it in the sepulchre."

"And it was Joseph's own new tomb," added a little girl. "He wasn't afraid then, for everybody must have known."

"I am sure he was very brave after that," said Mr. Watkins, looking pleased at the interest of the children. "Now, tell me what kind of a tomb it was."

"It was hewn out of a rock, I suppose, like a cave," said one.

"It had a door, with a stone to shut it up," said another.

"The door was low, I know, because the disciple stooped down to look in," said another.

"Yes, and the angel sat on it, too."

"All good answers," said Mr. Watkins. "The tomb was like a cave, probably had two divisions, and a kind of entrance court, the body of Jesus being laid in the inner part.

Now here are two pictures, one of them represents a tomb out in the middle of a garden, with little walks and flowers. The tomb is like a long, straight marble box ; the cover is lifted; there are two angels and several persons standing around it.

"The other picture is also a garden. There are no regular walks, but a good many trees and fewer flowers, though those that are there are bright and beautiful. One side seems rocky, like the side of a hill, and in it there is a low opening as into a cave, which seems light inside. On a stone, beside the door, an angel is seated, several persons— men and women—are also standing around. These two pictures are copied from large ones, representing the tomb of Jesus Christ. They are painted just as the artists *thought* the tomb looked. Which one do you think is nearest right ?"

They all exclaimed, " The **one** with the rocky side !"

" Why do you think so ?" asked Mr. Watkins.

"Because that is nearest to what the Bible says."

"Who can say the words?"

Nearly all the children answered: "Joseph laid Him in a sepulchre, which was hewn out of a rock, and rolled a stone unto the door of the sepulchre."

"That is right. Now, whenever you see what is called a Bible-picture, read the description in the Bible, and see if the person who drew the picture, made it like the account that is given.

"What took place very early in the morning at the end of the Sabbath?"

"There was a great earthquake; for the angel of the Lord descended from heaven, and came and rolled back the stone from the door, and sat upon it."

"How could this have been done in the morning, and also at 'the end of the Sabbath?'"

Henry answered: "The Jewish days began in the afternoon, and ended the next morning, sir, so that the end of the Sabbath was the morning of the first day of the week."

" Right," said Mr. Watkins. " Now tell me about the appearance of the angel ?"

" ' His countenance was like lightning, and his raiment white as snow.' "

" Is there any description of the appearance of our Lord, as He rose from the tomb ?"

" No, sir, I don't think any one saw Him rise. The keepers were like dead men, they were so frightened at the angel, and no one was there till afterwards."

" Who came first to the sepulchre ?"

" Mary Magdalene, and the other Mary."

" Yes, they came first, ' and spices brought and sweet perfume.' Let us sing about ' Mary to the Saviour's tomb,' and then we will go on :

> " Mary to the Saviour's tomb
>   Hasted at the early dawn:
> Spice she brought, and sweet perfume,
>   But the Lord she loved was gone.
> For awhile, she lingering stood,
>   Fill'd with sorrow and surprise ;

Trembling, while a crystal flood
    Issued from her weeping eyes.

"But her sorrows quickly fled,
    When she heard His welcome voice.
Christ had risen from the dead !
    Now He bids her heart rejoice.
What a change His word can make
    Turning darkness into day !
Ye who weep for Jesus' sake,
    He will wipe your tears away."

This beautiful hymn was sung by the children, and then Mr. Watkins continued.

"How did they know that the body of Jesus was not in the sepulchre ?"

"'They entered in, and found not the body of Jesus.'"

"What did they think about it ?"

"They did not know what to think, they were 'perplexed' about it."

"Who told them that Jesus had risen ?"

"Two men stood by them in shining garments, and said : 'Why seek ye the living among the dead ? He is not here, but is risen.'"

" How did the angel prove that Jesus was not in the tomb ?"

" He told them to come in and see."

" Right, but I want the words of St. Mark."

" 'Be not affrighted : Ye seek Jesus of Nazareth, which was crucified. He is risen ; He is not here : behold the place where they laid Him.' "

" To whom did the angel say this ?"

" To the Marys."

" What else did he tell them ?"

" Go your way, tell His disciples and Peter that He goeth before you into Galilee : there ye shall see Him."

" Who told Peter about what had taken place ?"

" Mary Magdalene."

" Who was with Peter ?"

" John, whom Jesus loved."

" Please repeat the words of St. John, beginning with the verse that tells of Mary Magdalene meeting them."

" 'Then she runneth, and cometh to Simon

Peter, and to the other disciple, whom Jesus loved, and saith unto them, They have taken away the Lord out of the sepulchre, and we know not where they have laid Him.'"

"Do you think she understood that Jesus had risen ?"

"No, sir, she thought the body had been taken somewhere else."

"What did Peter and that other disciple do ?"

"'They ran both together : and that other disciple did outrun Peter, and came first to the sepulchre.'"

"What did St. John do ?"

"'He, stooping down, and looking in, saw the linen clothes lying ; yet went he not in.'"

"What did St. Peter do ?"

"'Then cometh Simon Peter following him, and went into the sepulchre, and seeth the linen clothes lie, and the napkin, that was about His head, not lying with the linen clothes, but wrapped together in a place by itself.'"

"Did St. John go in after this?"

"'Then went in that other disciple, which came first to the sepulchre, and he saw, and believed."

"What did he believe?"

"That Jesus had risen from the dead."

"Why had they required so much evidence to convince them?"

"'For as yet they knew not the Scripture, that He must rise again from the dead.'"

"What is the meaning of 'knew not'?"

"Did not entirely understand."

"Where did the disciples then go?"

"Unto their own home."

"If they had staid a little longer, whom might they have seen?"

"Jesus, who had risen."

"Repeat the verse which tells of His speaking to Mary."

"'Jesus saith unto her, Mary. She turned herself, and said unto Him, Rabboni; which is to say, Master.'"

"Now, dear children, we have heard some

of the facts, relating to the rising of our Lord.
We have not time to repeat every one of them.
No one saw the actual uprising of that body
which had been wound in fine linen ; no one
but the angels who ministered unto Him. We
only know that he left the grave clothes, as
He did the tomb, and walked again upon the
earth among His disciples, until He was taken
from them into Heaven.

"Who knows how long our Lord remained
on earth ?"

"Forty days, sir."

"Where do you find that ?"

"In the first chapter of Acts, third verse."

"Read it aloud, if you please."

" 'To whom also He showed Himself alive
after His passion, by many infallible proofs,
being seen of them forty days, and speaking of
the things pertaining to the kingdom of God.'"

"Yes, forty days they saw Him and heard
Him, and then He rose from earth, to the
right hand of God the Father. What do we
call the day on which He was taken up ?"

" Ascension-day."

" Right; and for the Sunday after Ascension-day, I want you to learn all you can about it. If you learn it as well as you have learned this lesson, I shall feel you have done the very best you could. I will ask you a few questions about the hymn, which will finish our exercises."

Mr. Watkins then read the first verse :

> " Christ the Lord is risen to-day,
> Sons of men and angels say :
> Raise your joys and triumphs high,
> Sing, ye heavens, and earth reply."

"What is the subject of this verse ?" he asked.

" The rising of Christ."

" Who and what are called upon to rejoice ?"

" Sons of men and angels," answered several voices, and then hesitated.

" What besides men and angels ?" he repeated.

" The heavens and the earth," said Henry, very plainly.

"Yes, all creation, the whole universe, is called upon to rejoice because the Lord hath risen. This reminds me of that magnificent song of Moses, which calls upon the universe in the same way: 'Give ear, oh ye heavens, and hear, oh earth; ascribe ye greatness unto our God.' And *we* now would ascribe greatness unto *our* God. So we sing, 'Christ the Lord hath risen to-day.'

> " 'Love's redeeming work is done,
> Fought the fight, the victory won:
> Jesus' agony is o'er,
> Darkness veils the earth no more.'

"Now, children, I want to know the meaning of that first line. What is the 'redeeming work,' referred to?"

"Christ's redeeming the world," answered several.

"How was this 'Love's redeeming work?'"

"Because Christ loved us." There was some hesitation about this answer, so Mr. Watkins repeated first John iii. 16: " 'Hereby perceive we the love of God, because He laid down

His life for us.' It was because He first loved us that Christ came to die for us. When was this 'redeeming work done?'"

"When Jesus was crucified," said one.

"When Jesus said, 'It is finished,' said another.

"Yes, dear children, then it was *done*. Now tell me, when was it *begun?*"

"When Christ was born."

"No, before that."

Henry remembered what Mr. Wordin had told them, and, after a moment's thought, said: "As soon as there was sin."

"Right; as soon as there was sin, then a Saviour was needed, and then Christ's work began. Sacrifices were offered then, to tell of the work of the coming Saviour. The Christians looked *forward* then, now we look *backward* to the sacrifice which was once offered. He fought the fight with sin, He gained the victory, His agony is over, and light and hope are spread over the earth.

      " ' Vain the stone, the watch, the seal,
        Christ hath burst the gates of hell ;
        Death in vain forbids Him rise :
        Christ hath opened Paradise.'

"What stone is meant ?"

Mary had been trying to gain courage to answer alone, and this time determined to do so. With a trembling voice, she said : "The stone which was at the door of the sepulchre."

"Yes, that stone had no power to keep Jesus in the tomb. What does 'the watch' mean ?"

"The Roman guard," said several voices.

"Right; only too few of you answer these questions. Now all try. What was the seal ?"

"The fastening of the stone."

"Yes, and it was probably made of clay or wax, and with a stamp upon it, so that it would be found out if it were broken. The 'gates of hell,' refers to the spiritual world which had no power to keep the spirit of our Lord from returning to His body, and rising from the tomb.

"'Soar we now where Christ hath led,
    Following our exalted Head;
    Made like Him, like Him we rise:
    Ours the cross, the grave, the skies.'

"What is told us in the beginning of this verse?"

"That we shall be like Him, and see Him as He is," said one of the older girls.

"Yes, that is true, like Him now, in that we shall rise again, like Him in sorrow, in death, and in that 'where He is, there shall we be also.' Now we will sing this hymn."

When the singing was over, Mr. Wordin prayed for them all, and then closed the exercises.

They had a delightful walk home, and each one had a heart full of joy as each one remembered the promise of the day:

"RESURGAM."

XXIV.

The End.

IDA and her mother went away together after dinner, for Ida's heart was full of a new joy. Nothing could have made her so happy, as the knowledge that her parents really understood old Mariano's goodness, and were not ashamed of him, but were grateful to him. It was enough, the child's heart was won, and she longed to tell the mother and father, who had sought for her so many years, that they had truly found their child.

Ida was much older in thought than in years, and quite able to explain to her mother, that the one drop which had been wanting in her cup of happiness had filled it now.

We will not listen to what passed in that hour, but after it, go with them to the nursery, for said Ida : " You do not really know Minny yet, dear mother."

" Minny," said Mrs. Dorris, " I want to thank you for all you have done for my little girl."

" You's berry welcome, Mis Dorris," said Minny. " I ain't done much for Miss Ida 'cept to praise de Lord for His blessing, in bringing her father and mother ober to dis land."

" Thank you for that, Minny. I feel that we do not thank the Lord as we ought."

" Blessings on you, Mis Dorris. I 'spect you's right, dat's where de trouble is. We tank de Lord when we is happy, and we prays and cries when we is miserable, and don't tank no more. I 'spect we orter tank jest de same all de time. De good Lord died jest de same, we can tank Him for dat. De good Lord rose from de tomb jest de same, we can tank Him for dat. De good Lord is a watching ober us, and a caring for us, and a helping us up when we fall down, and a forgiving us when we sin, jest de same. 'Pears like we neber orter stop a tanking and a praising."

"You are right, Minny, and yet I almost forgot to thank Him for anything when my child was lost."

"Yes, Mis Dorris, you see we isn't berry 'trong,and you jest forgot dat de Lord had dat chile. She was nebber lost, real true, sure."

"She was lost to me," said Mrs. Dorris, with a shudder.

"Yes, missis, dat's true, but dat was 'cause you is down on dis ground, and couldn't see all ober, like de Lord, who libs up so high. He heard de prayer eben widout de praises. He took care ob de little lamb. He nebber lets His lambs go 'stray for long."

"But, Minny, how can you be happy about *everything?*" asked Ida.

"Don' know, Miss Ida. I has so many tings to be thankful for, dat de oder tings gets crowded out. I prays for de sins dat de people in de dark does. Dem as has deir eyes shut, 'cause dere ain't *really* no dark anywhere. De good Lord is de light ob de

world. Den I prays for de sick folks, and for
de animals ; dem you know as has hard masters,
and no afterwards to make it up to dem.
Dat's what I prays for. I don't want notin'
myself. My child'n's in de light ob glory, all
safe in de hebbenly Master's arms. I has
more dan I wants in dis life, and

" I'se going, I'se going to de hebbenly land,
So I'll sing, so I'll sing,
Josus, hallelujah !

"So den dere I'll be happy in de Master's hand,
Praises ring, Praises ring,
Jesus, hallelujah !

" Dere in de glory dere is sinning nebbermore,
Den I'll sing, Den I'll sing,
Jesus, hallelujah !

"Dere de stars make de sand ob hebben's shiny shore
Praises ring, Praises ring,
Jesus, hallelujah !"

Minny ceased, and closed her eyes, as if she
saw the home that " hath no need of the sun,
neither of the moon to shine in it, for the
glory of God did lighten it, and the Lamb
is the light thereof."

"Minny, I thank you for what you have said to me this night. I trust I will never be ungrateful again, but serve my Master better every day," said Mrs. Dorris, taking Minny's hand, gratefully.

"Good-night, dear Minny," said Ida.

After leaving the nursery, they rejoined the family, and the remainder of the evening was passed in cheerful conversation on the events not only of the day, but on those of that first glorious Easter which had made man's hope a faith.

Before separating for the night, they united in singing the beautiful old hymn :

"Awake, my soul, to joyful lays,
And sing thy great Redeemer's praise :
He justly claims a song from thee ;
His loving-kindness, oh, how free !

"When trouble, like a gloomy cloud,
Has gathered thick and thundered loud,
He near my soul has always stood ;
His loving-kindness, oh, how good !

"Sometimes I feel my sinful heart,
Prone from my Saviour to depart ;

But though I oft have Him forgot,
His loving-kindness changes not.

"Then let me mount and soar away,
To the bright world of endless day,
And sing with rapture and surprise,
His loving-kindness in the skies."

THE END.

This is all I can tell you now about Henry and Mary and Ida, but I want you to learn from this little story, first and last, to love the Lord Jesus Christ with your whole hearts, that there may ever be to your lives a

BRIGHTSIDE.